# The World As Light

# The World As Light

## An Introduction to the Art of

# Adi Da Samraj

by Mei-Ling Israel

Da Plastique™

Book design: Matt Barna

Published by Da Plastique (www.daplastique.com; info@daplastique.com)
and The Dawn Horse Press, Middletown, California.

Printed in the USA

International Standard Book Number: 978-1-57097-230-0
Library of Congress Control Number: 2007928146

# CONTENTS

# INTRODUCTION

BY JONATHAN CONDIT

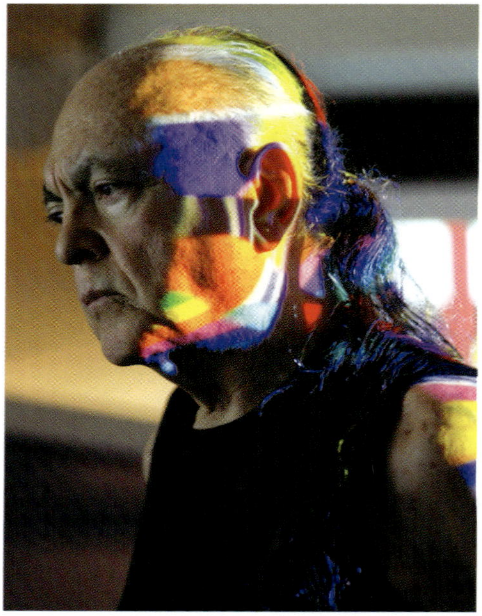

Deeply involved in the artistic process since childhood, Adi Da Samraj has, in the last nine years, created a massive body of highly distinctive and highly diverse work. In that nine-year period, he has "stretched" the medium of photography—and also the medium of videography—in many directions. Most recently, he has begun to develop remarkable new potentials in the digital medium.

Adi Da's collateral exhibition at the 52nd Biennale di Venezia (2007) marks the first time his work is being shown to the global art public. The Biennale exhibition is devoted to his most recent works, from 2006–2007. The purpose of *The World As Light* is to provide an overview of his entire artistic oeuvre of the past forty years—accompanied by key statements he has made on his own art and on the artistic process in general.

Adi Da Samraj regards his art as building upon the modernist tradition. He greatly values the radical aesthetic freedom and the profundity of meaning characteristic of modernism at its best. And he intends his own art to convey the deepest of meanings—relative to the nature of the human situation, and relative to the nature of reality altogether.

As Adi Da makes clear, his art can be "read" as an immense investigation of the human condition—the condition of presumed existence as a "self" in the midst of a world that is "not-self". Adi Da's art is meant to call into question the most basic presumptions of ordinary human life: the "fact" of existing as an independent "self", the "fact" of every "self" being separate from every other "self", the "fact" of the "self" being separate from the world of "everything else". Indeed, Adi Da intends his art to communicate the profundity that is known when all presumptions of "separateness" are relinquished.

The condition of non-separateness—as the true nature of the human situation, and the true nature of reality altogether—is the core of Adi Da's communication. He makes this communication not only as an artist, but also as one who has given an entirely new process by which the illusion of separateness can be gone beyond.

Adi Da himself has always lived and demonstrated non-separateness. His entire life has been a manifestation of uniquely profound spiritual illumination. And his constant effort has been to fully communicate the way of non-separateness—through his many published writings and discourses, and through his many works of image-art.

In his book *Transcendental Realism*, Adi Da declares:

> Reality Itself <u>Is</u> Truth Itself <u>Is</u> The Beautiful Itself.

Ultimately, this is the vision he intends to convey through his art. Thus, he offers his art to the world as his communication of reality and truth—and, also, as an address to the "human necessity" for the "aesthetic experience of real and true beauty".

Jonathan Condit is senior editor of the Dawn Horse Press.

# Absolute Light

## A Prologue in the Words and Pictures of Adi Da Samraj

*My images are created to be a means*
*for any and every perceiving, feeling,*
*and fully participating viewer*
*to "Locate" Fundamental and Really Perfect Light—*

*the world* <u>*As*</u> *Light,*
*all relations* <u>*As*</u> *Light,*
*conditional (or naturally perceived) light*
<u>*As*</u> *Absolute Light.*

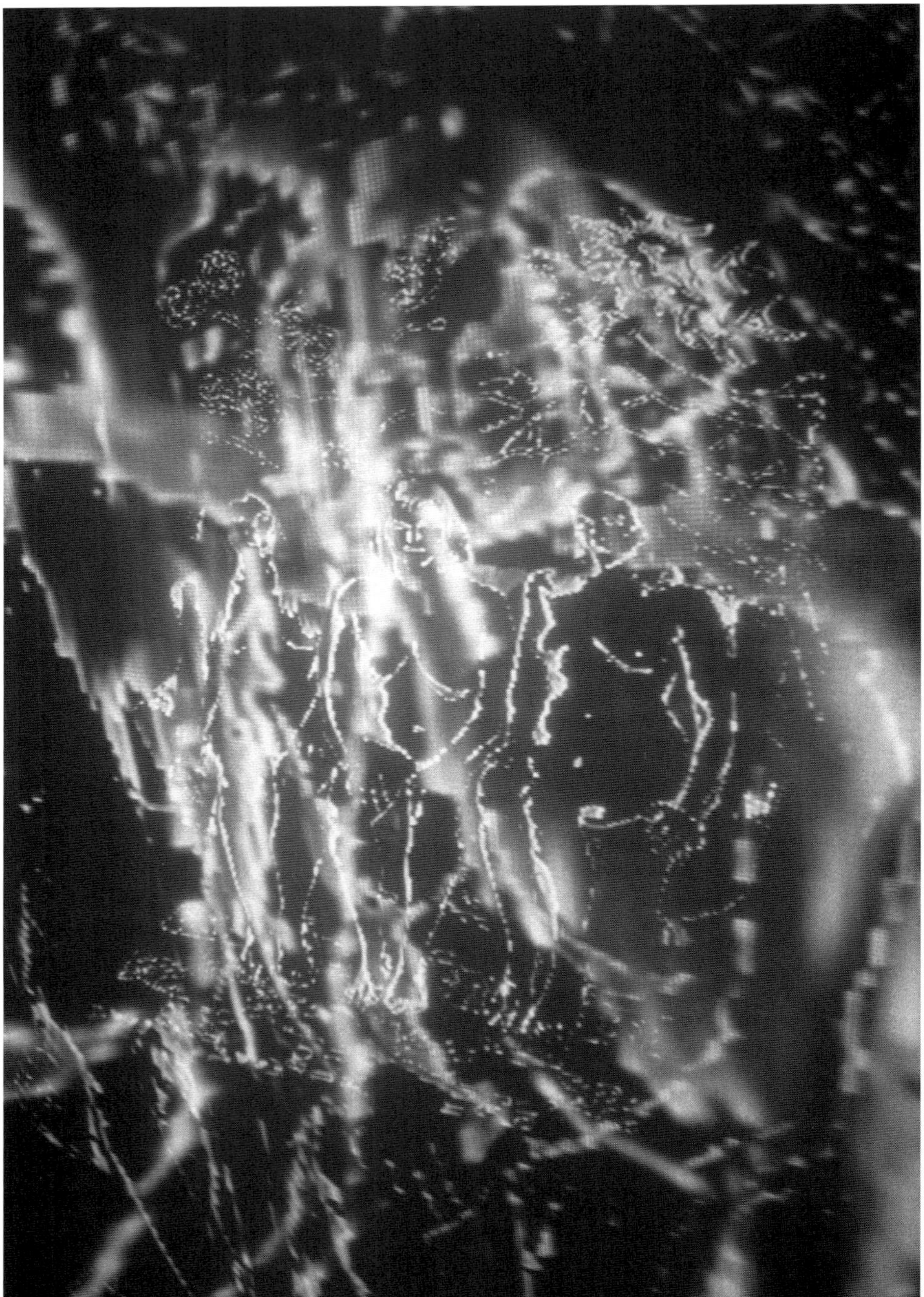

Black-and-white photograph (multiple-exposed in camera), 2001.
From the Suite *Odalisque: The Myth of the Reclining Woman.*

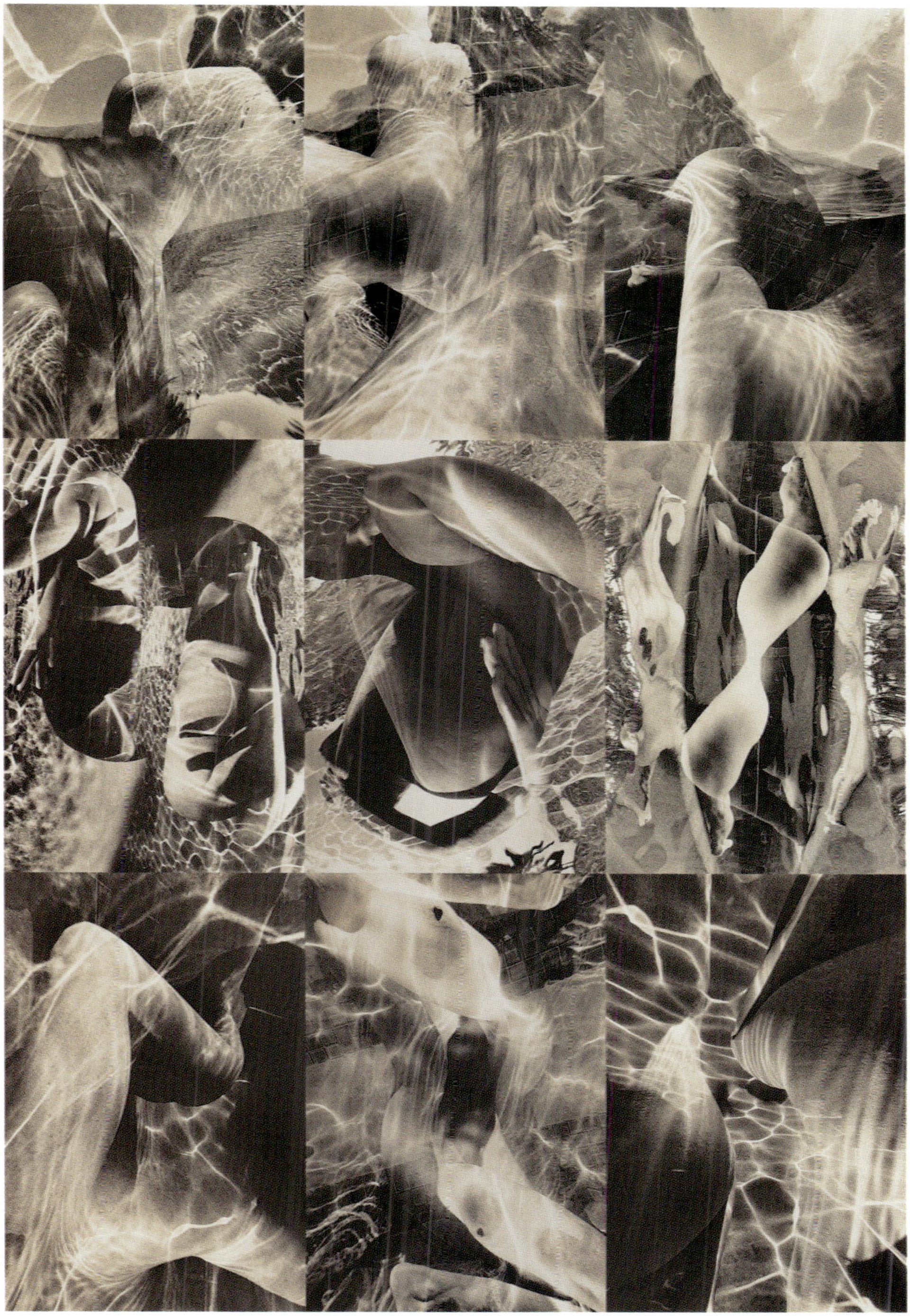

*Quandra Loka #202*. A configuration of nine sepia-toned photographs (each photograph multiple-exposed in camera), 2002.
From the Suite *Quandra Loka: The Indivisible Space of Conscious Light*.

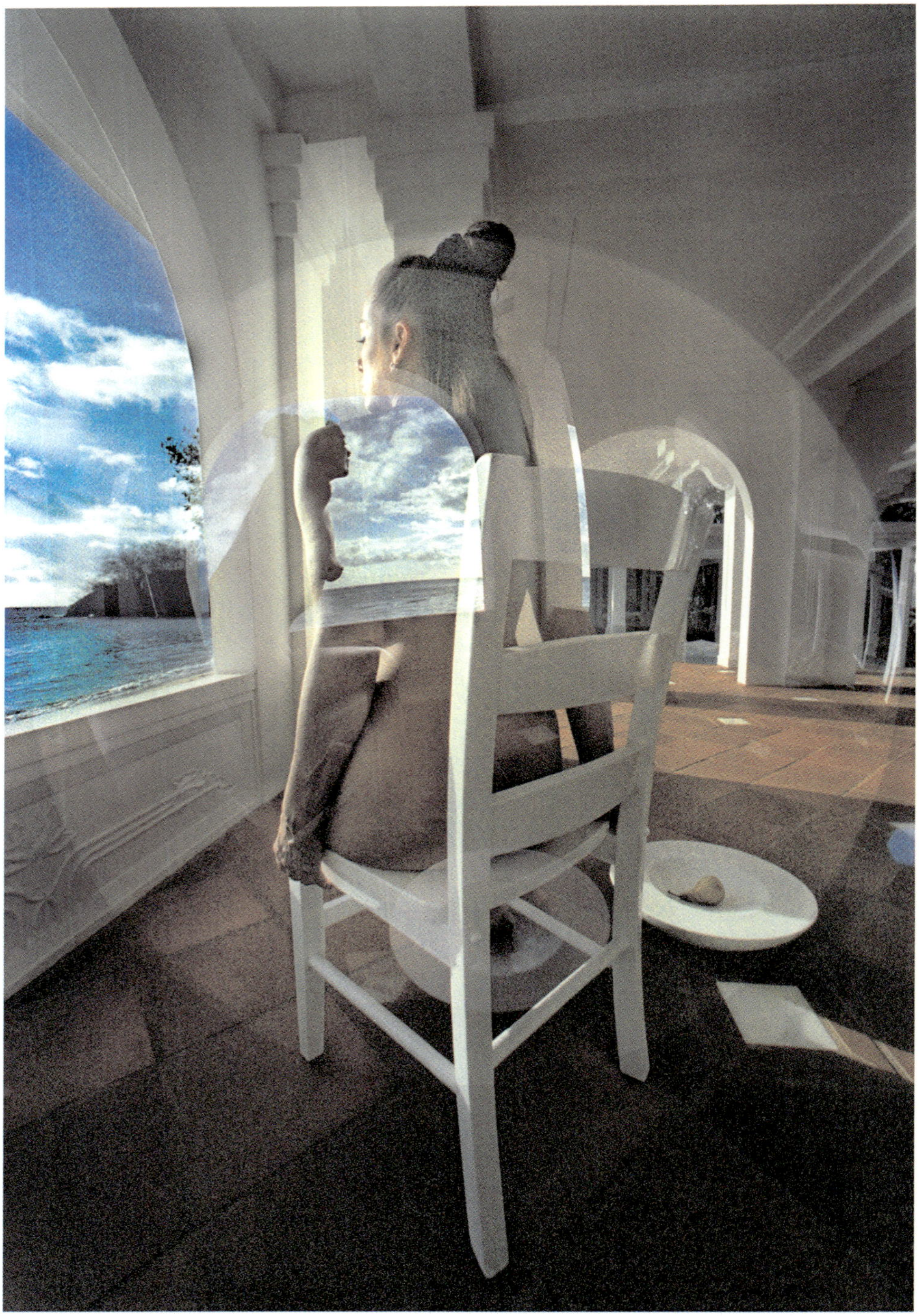

Color photograph (multiple-exposed in camera), 2003.
From the Suite *The Spherical Tower.*

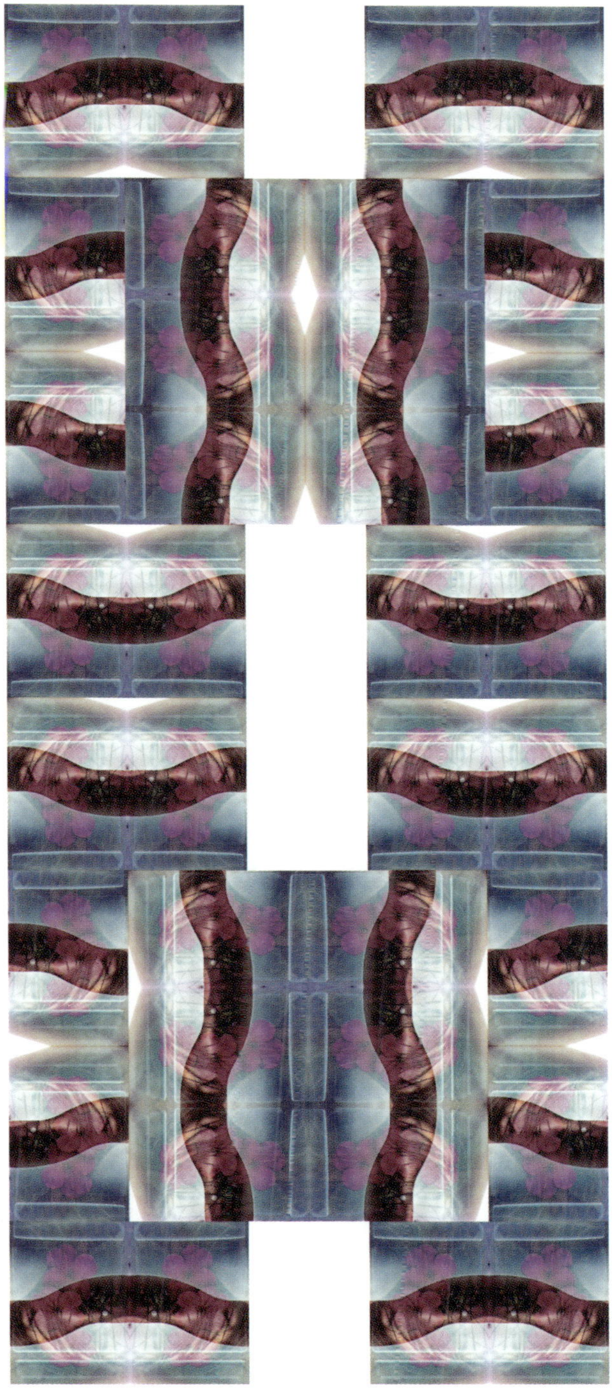

A configuration of thirty-six "cells" of the same color photograph (multiple-exposed in camera), 2003.
From the Suite *Kaleidoscape: Eleven Visions of Countless Points of View.*

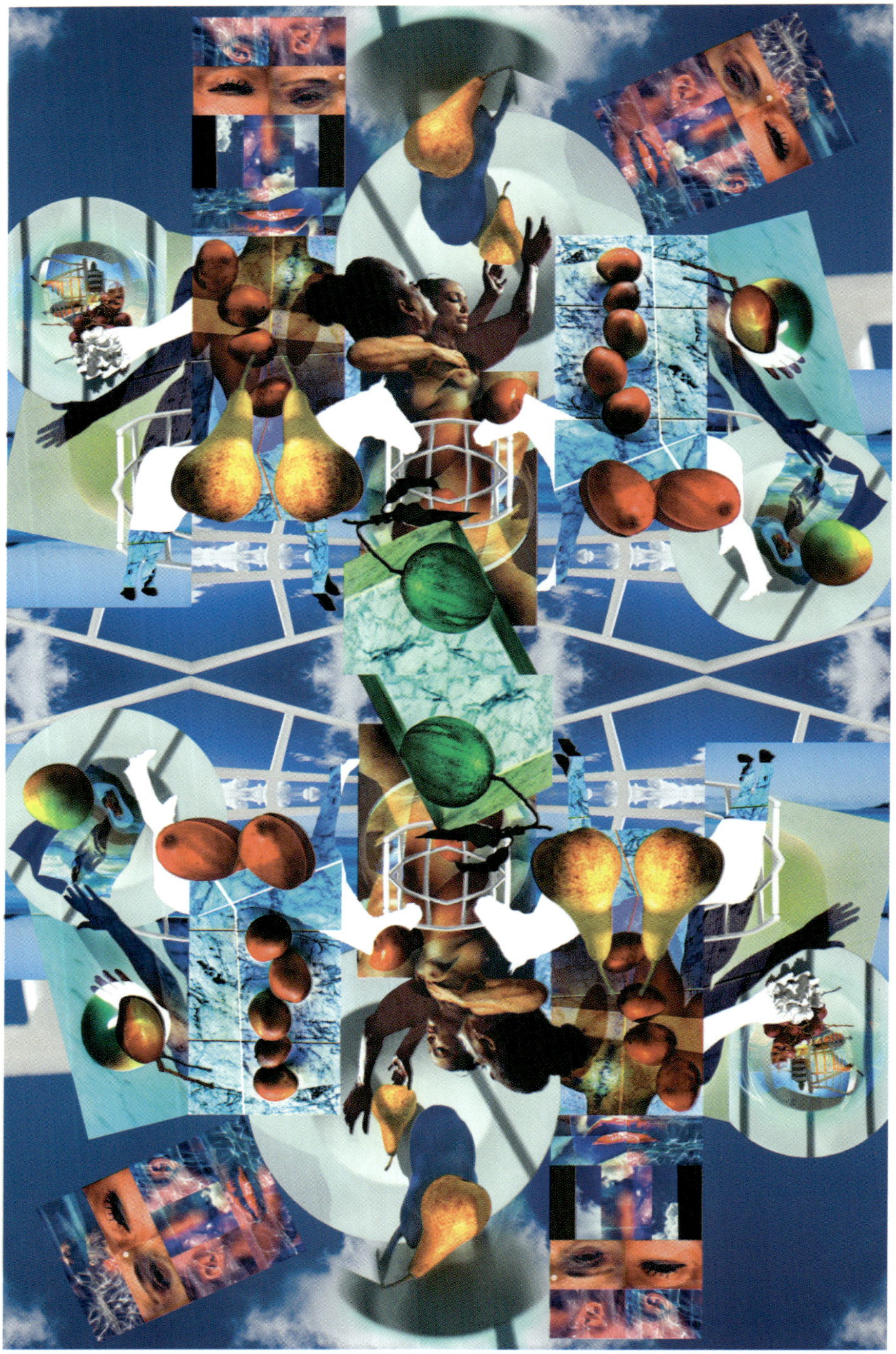

Digitally-constructed Image (incorporating multiple-exposed photographic elements), 2006.
From the Suite *Spectra Three: Quandra Contemplating the Fruits of Perfect Knowledge.*

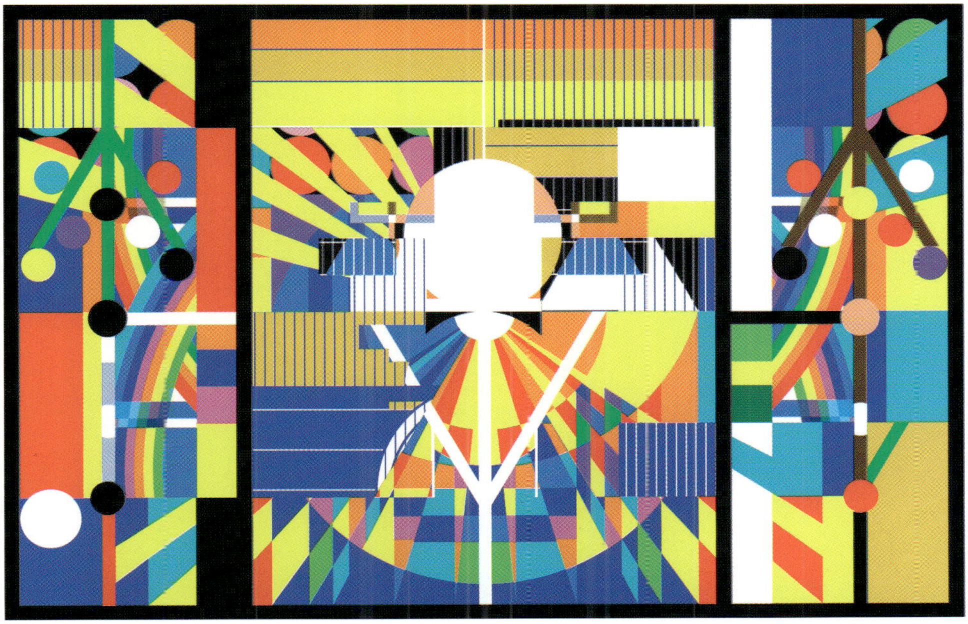

Sunday 4

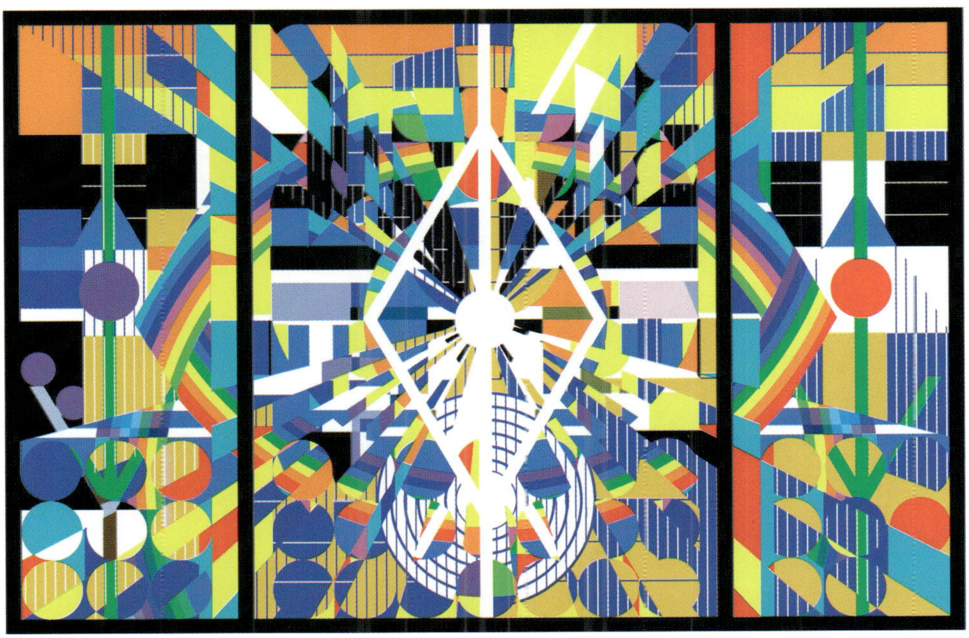

Monday 4

Digitally-constructed Images, 2006.
From the Suite *Geome One: Alberti's Window*,
Part One: *The Order Of The Day*.

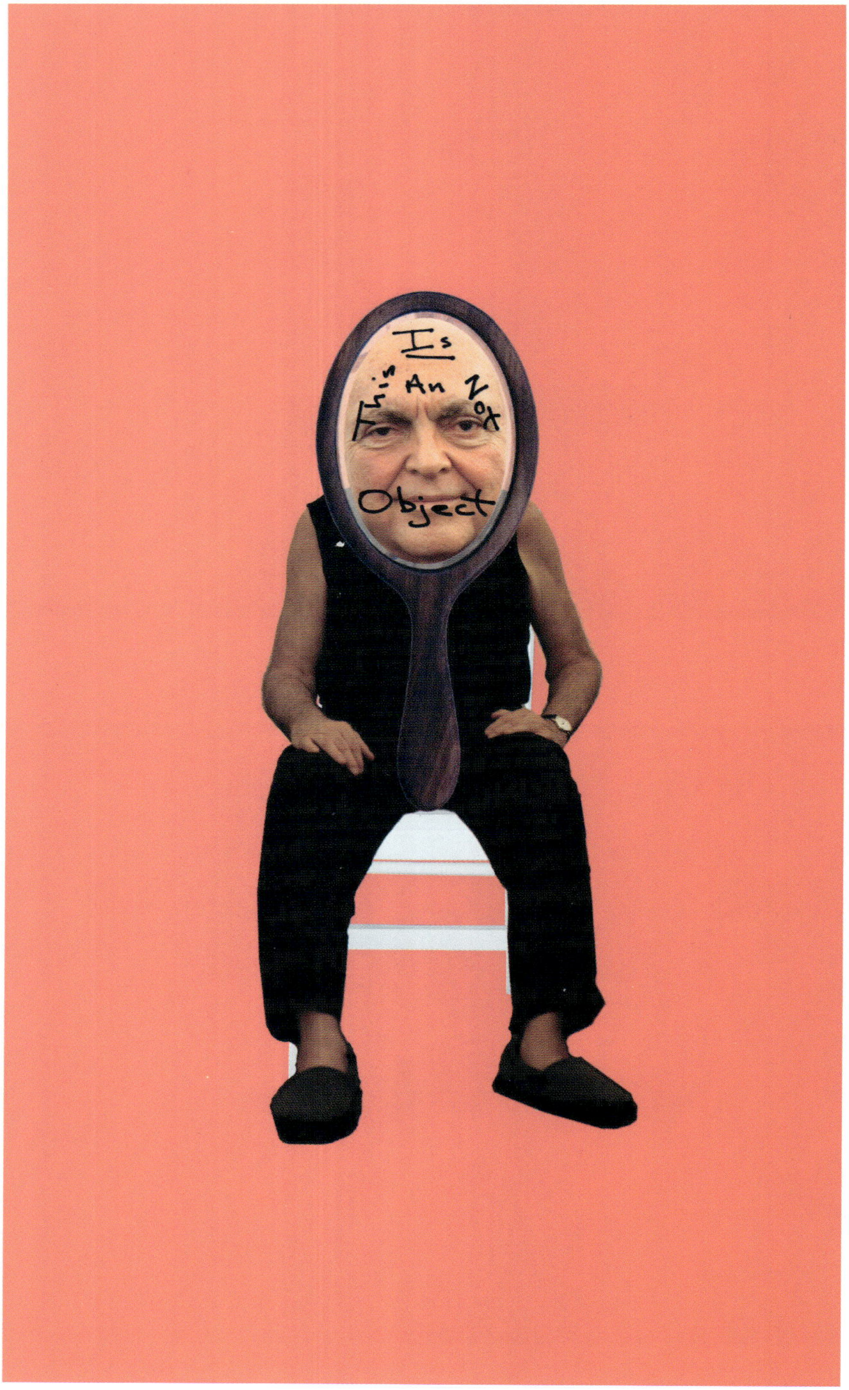


*Portrait Of The Artist <u>As</u> Not-An-Object 3*, 2006.
From *The Perfect Mirror Three.*

CHAPTER ONE

# The "Room" Beyond "Point of View"

## Looking in the Mirror

Adi Da Samraj has often spoken of the Greek myth of Narcissus, who stared into his own reflection in the pond, as a metaphor for the essence of human suffering. Narcissus falls in love with the beautiful face in the water, believing it is someone else. He is so spellbound by his own reflection that he never even hears the voice of his true beloved, and he eventually wastes away and dies.

When Adi Da tells this story, he calls attention to the water itself—the "real" place in which the illusory reflection appears. Carrying this lesson into his art, the reflective water is sometimes depicted as a mirror. The image on the facing page, from his *Perfect Mirror* suites, can be seen as a visual "artist's statement". This paradoxical work, *Portrait Of The Artist <u>As</u> Not-An-Object*, holds the key to the purpose and meaning of all of Adi Da's images.

While reminiscent of Magritte, Adi Da goes beyond the surrealistic play with objective meaning. "This <u>Is</u> Not An Object" is a directive to the viewer. He is saying: Look in the mirror, and instead of seeing a separate "other", keep looking beyond this illusion, to the mirror itself. If you take this instruction, you go through the mirror, and enter the "room"—a place of no distinction between subject and object, a place of non-separate unity. This is Adi Da's gift to those who truly view his art.

Adi Da also describes the illusion of Narcissus as "point of view". In Adi Da's language, "point of view" is the error of looking at the world from a position in time and space, where "you" are at the center. "Point of view" is all that prevents entrance to the "room" of seamlessness and liberation from the pain of separateness.

## Seeing the "Room"

Throughout his life, Adi Da has been asking the question, "What would the room look like if it were viewed from all possible 'points of view' at once?" How, in other words, could the totality of reality be known, without any involvement in the illusion of separation?

*Reality itself—like the "room" itself, as it is—is beyond "point of view". You always see every "room" from your "point of view". But the "room" exists, otherwise, as it is—from every possible "point of view" in space-time. Where is that "room"? Where are you in that "room"?**

This is the purpose of Adi Da's art: to reveal the "room" beyond "point of view". This is also why he calls his art "Transcendental Realism"—because his art is purposed to show the true nature of reality, instead of what reality merely appears to be. Adi Da's own creative act, beyond "point of view", is what allows reality to be revealed in his images.

*The artistic work I do is a way of breaking beyond the limits of the separative body-mind, or the ego. It is about transcending the body-mind and transcending the ego by being entered into the root-dimension—which is that dimension of experiencing that is in touch with the real situation of existence. That is how the images are made. That is what they are about. The profundity of transcending the ego is what all the imagery I make is about.*

## Unguarded Participation

Adi Da describes his art not as an object, but as a "performance-assisted subjective process". By this, he means that each viewer is assisted in the unique process of transcending "point of view", via an art "performed" in freedom.

In his essay "The Beautiful Room of Perfect Space", from his book *Transcendental Realism: The Image-Art of egoless Coincidence with Reality Itself*,** Adi Da speaks of the "true and traditional" purpose of

*Unless otherwise indicated, all quotations from Adi Da Samraj are taken from transcripts of his audio-recorded commentaries on his art, and on art in general, as these have been given in the period from the 1980s to the present.

**Published by the Dawn Horse Press (Middletown, CA: 2007).

the arts. It is to draw the human being into the "sphere of the 'aesthetic experience'—in which the entire brain and nervous system . . . is profoundly 'tuned' to Reality". He says this state is identical to the "aesthetic experience of beauty", and calls it a great and necessary "human profundity", which "true art must serve".

The purity of the aesthetic experience actually requires no words, no concepts. As Adi Da has said, art speaks for itself. The secret in receiving Adi Da's art, therefore, is unguarded participation, allowing the aesthetically tuned faculties of the brain and nervous system to do their work, rather than letting the mind be a barrier to what is apparently incomprehensible. As Adi Da has said, his images are intended to function as a means for the "brain to outgrow its illusions". His art is a response to a universal human need.

*The images I make invite people to a participatory and transformative process. My images serve a mode of participation and perception that is non-ordinary, that breaks beyond the "box" of the body-mind. "Point of view", or the ego's mode of viewing existence, is gone beyond, undermined—not "flattered", not permitted, in some sense—by the very nature of these images.*

*I work to have the images serve the participant's transformative participation in reality altogether, to draw the participant into sublimity.*

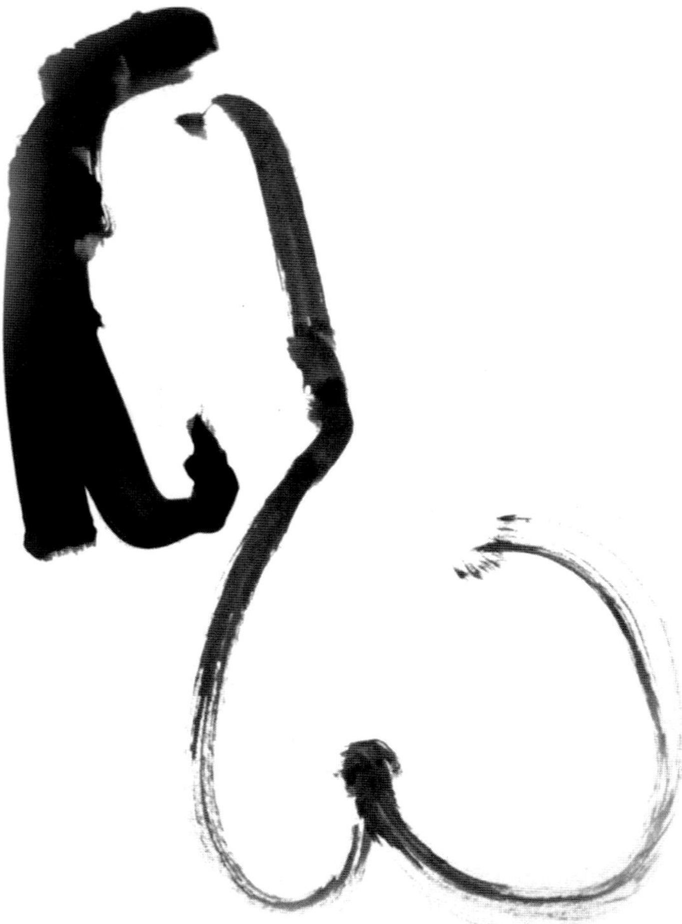

Transcendental Drawing, 1967.
Later given the title *Woman in Mind*. Brush and ink on paper.

CHAPTER TWO

# Subject and Meaning

## The Discovery of a Method

Adi Da sees his artistic life-work as a continuity, his decades of image-making rooted in a single approach. From drawing to painting to photography to digital media, Adi Da has always animated this principle. Both an artistic method and a philosophy, Adi Da calls his primary impulse "a complete investment in the subject". This relationship is the basis for meaning in all his images.

Adi Da first discovered his artistic life-method in a life-drawing class taken at Columbia University in the late 1950s. In a class exercise known as "blind contour drawing", he suddenly found a freedom in relating to the subject only, without reference to the drawing surface.

*It was an approach in which I did not look at the hand that was doing the drawing. So the drawing I engaged was not about hand-eye coordination, or about looking at the surface, or the instrument, or the pots of paint, or the pens. My approach became entirely about regarding the subject, a complete investment in the subject.*

*The subject was a nude—a human being just as is, without the social characteristics imparted by clothing. I realized I could simply be totally given over to perceptual participation in the subject. Thus, I began to develop, in very basic terms, an approach in which I could physically sense everything I needed to sense about the surface, the paints, the instruments in hand. I could be physically aware of them in a spatial and tactile sense, such that I did not have to look at those things—or, at most, I would occasionally re-orient with just a glance. Instead, I was constantly remaining physically oriented to the subject.*

*I have worked in this manner ever since. I invest in this work with the whole body, not merely with a part of it—such that neither the wrist, nor the conceptual mind, nor mere perception controls or manages the plastic form.*

This method—of being entirely attentive to the subject—is the basis of all forms of Adi Da's art to this day. Consequently, he requires the medium to be a fluid extension of his body, never impeding his participatory response to the subject. The ability to maintain the disposition of non-separateness from the subject became the first distinctive development in Adi Da's intention to go beyond "point of view" via his art.

# The Necessity of Meaning

In addition to his studio-art studies, Adi Da's time at Columbia afforded him in-depth study of the modernist tradition in art, literature, and music—as well as in his major area of study, philosophy. Years later, he said, "to be familiar with the entire artistic and literary tradition of the West was part of the discipline I embraced by which I prepared to make literature and artistic imagery".

In the modernist painters—such as Cézanne, Kandinsky, Picasso, and others—Adi Da found what he has called a "liberating instant" in the history of art. His subsequent Stanford master's thesis became a pivotal investigation into the capacity for abstract art to communicate meaning. This study, later titled *The Reduction Of The Beloved To Shape Alone: The Effort Toward Abstraction, The Pure Present, and The New In "Modern" Art, Psychology, and Philosophy—Especially As Defined In The "Meaningless" Aesthetic Theories Of Gertrude Stein,** is his most important writing on art previous to *Transcendental Realism*, his seminal 2007 collection of essays.

Early in his thesis, Adi Da reveals his own purposes, as an artist and writer, in studying the writings of Gertrude Stein and her essential dilemma about the "problem of consciousness".

*It is appropriate to approach her work as we would a manifestation of our own enigma and suffering and artistic practice. We should seek to understand it if only to free ourselves and come to a true perception of aesthetic values.*

Adi Da then proceeds to measure Stein's success in her literary experiment. Like his life-drawing-class discovery, Adi Da's research into Gertrude Stein had a direct and permanent effect on the philosophical underpinnings of his artistic process. In the thesis, he considers, from a myriad of angles, whether her effort to reduce words to mere "plasticity" works. Adi Da acknowledges that her artistic fervor led her to a remarkable point of personal liberation. But while her art succeeded for her, he finds that it does not succeed in the same way for others. Exploiting verbal abstraction to such a degree made her experience of reality inaccessible to the reader, because meaning—the bridge for others to understand her state of consciousness—was missing.

**The Reduction Of The Beloved To Shape Alone* is as yet unpublished.

*To be sure, her work "worked" for her. . . . She underwent profound psychic growth. . . . The artist was whole . . . [but] the works are mad.*

The obligation to meaning, therefore, became the other critical development in the early years of Adi Da's artistic work. He champions the aesthetic experience itself, the art's origin in the subject, and the viewer's participation in the artwork as the elements essential to meaningful art.

*My visual artistic work is not about reducing visual forms to meaningless shapes. When images are just shapes or thing-ness, and that is as far as it goes, then there is nothing in which the viewer can participate. Such is a dead end. It is empty.*

*Meaning is a fundamental characteristic of plastic forms when they are used in the true artistic sense. Of course, meaning in art does not have to be literalistic—but if you simply evoke pattern without meaning, without drawing an individual into participation in the true aesthetic experience, there is no participation in true art.*

*When images are just about the "paint", they become mere "wallpaper". Art is not merely about pattern. It is not about mere color against color, line against line, shape against shape. Art is <u>meaning</u>. Meaning is the fundamental "substance" applied to the canvas or put on the page. Every kind of abstracting method possible—using whatever medium, verbal or perceptual—needs to be kept in the framework, the vocabulary, or the "room" of meaning.*

*Meaning is the discipline of art.*

## Transcendental Drawings

Very few of Adi Da's early artworks survive—due to a dramatic culmination of his creative process in 1965, when he chose to burn his entire body of drawings and manuscripts. It took him three full days to burn the entire corpus of literary and artistic materials—which he has estimated to be between fifteen and twenty thousand pages—in the fireplace of his New York apartment. As he writes in his autobiography, *The Knee Of Listening:*

*I was aware that something significant and creative might . . . be destroyed—but I knew, in any case, that whatever concrete results were produced . . . were retained in my mind. . . . What was substantial in all that I burned would remain in me, to be used whenever the real impulses of art were awakened. . . . Thus, I would be empty and creatively free.*

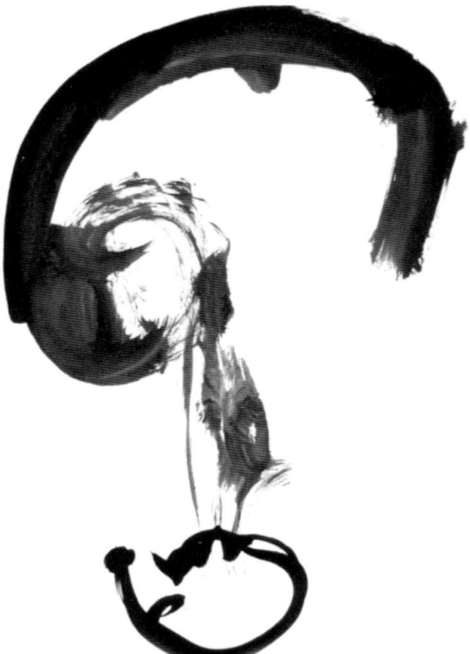

Transcendental Drawing, 1967.
Later given the title *Husband*. Brush and ink on paper.

Not long after the burning, Adi Da resumed his art of "total investment in the subject" with a series of ink brush drawings exhibited in 1967 at the Philadelphia Theological Seminary, where he was a student at the time. The drawings shown at this exhibition are his earliest surviving artwork (aside from a number of photographs he had taken in earlier years).

During the 1970s, Adi Da continued making such drawings at various times—most often while he was in the midst of speaking to a roomful of people. Adi Da would spontaneously pick up a clipboard of paper that he kept nearby and make a quick drawing, sometimes using only a ballpoint pen on yellow writing paper. As always, he maintained his method of total investment in the subject, barely glancing down while he drew. Spanning a period of over three decades, from the late 1960s to as recently as 2002, the drawings are a range of sizes and styles.

Adi Da later gave the name "Transcendental Drawings" to this body of work. By "transcendental", Adi Da is indicating his method of working beyond the usual presumption of separation between artist and subject—or between the "I" and what is perceived. The art, thus originating in a disposition that transcends "point of view", is meant to invite the viewer into the same state of freedom.

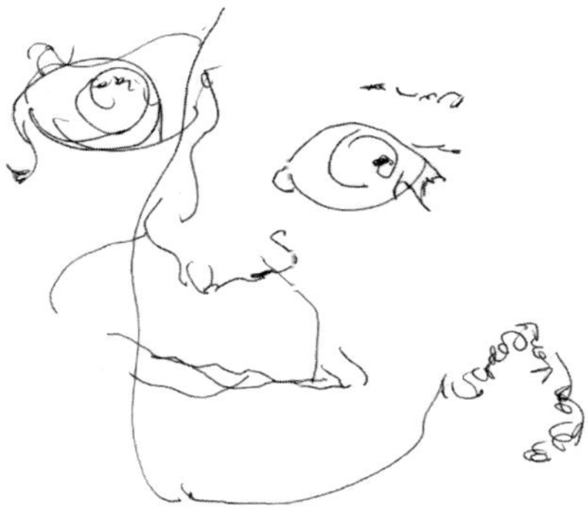

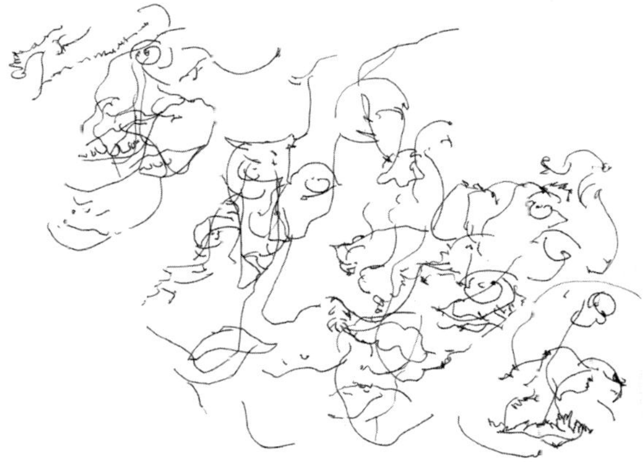

Transcendental Drawings, 1970s.
Pen on paper.

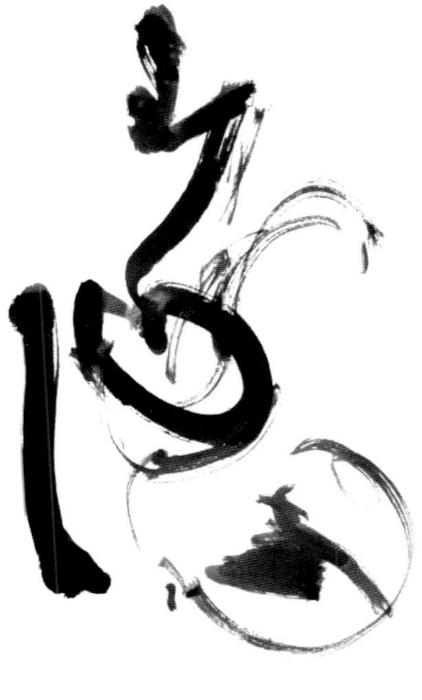

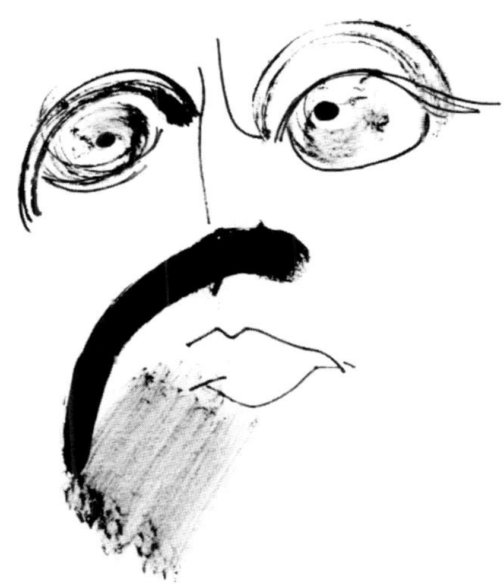

Transcendental Drawings, late 1960s.
Brush and ink on paper.

# Miniature Self-Portraits

No matter what material he employed or what circumstance he was in, Adi Da Samraj demonstrated a consistent purpose in his art, calling it, at one point, "a way of dealing with the formal existence of all relations without introducing a sense of separation".

Often Adi Da's relationships with those close to him inspired his artwork. In 1984, he had recently taken up residence on an island in Fiji (where he continues to live today). Over the coming year, Adi Da created forty-three miniature self-portraits—each about two inches high—using enamel paint, mostly in red, yellow, black, and white. He created the miniatures as birthday gifts for the small group in residence there.

While making these paintings, Adi Da had the person whose birthday it was sit directly in front of him, holding a hand mirror at chest-height. In the five to ten minutes it took him to make the portrait, Adi Da looked in the mirror, and briefly at the person holding the mirror—glancing only occasionally at the surface of the painting and his materials. Adi Da said each self-portrait was a "response" showing the person <u>as</u> himself, or a combination of himself and the person.

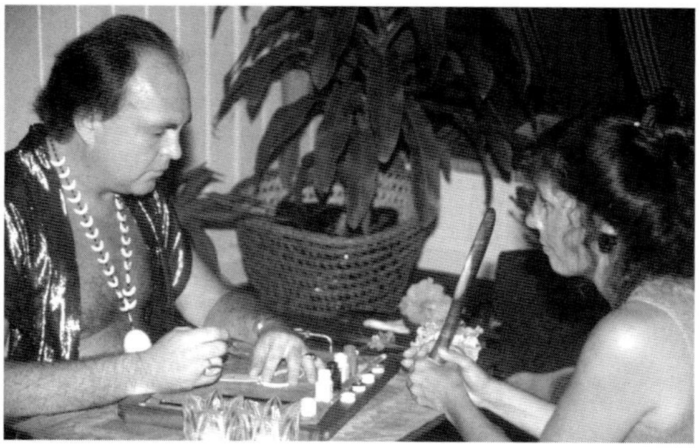

Adi Da Samraj painting a miniature self-portrait.

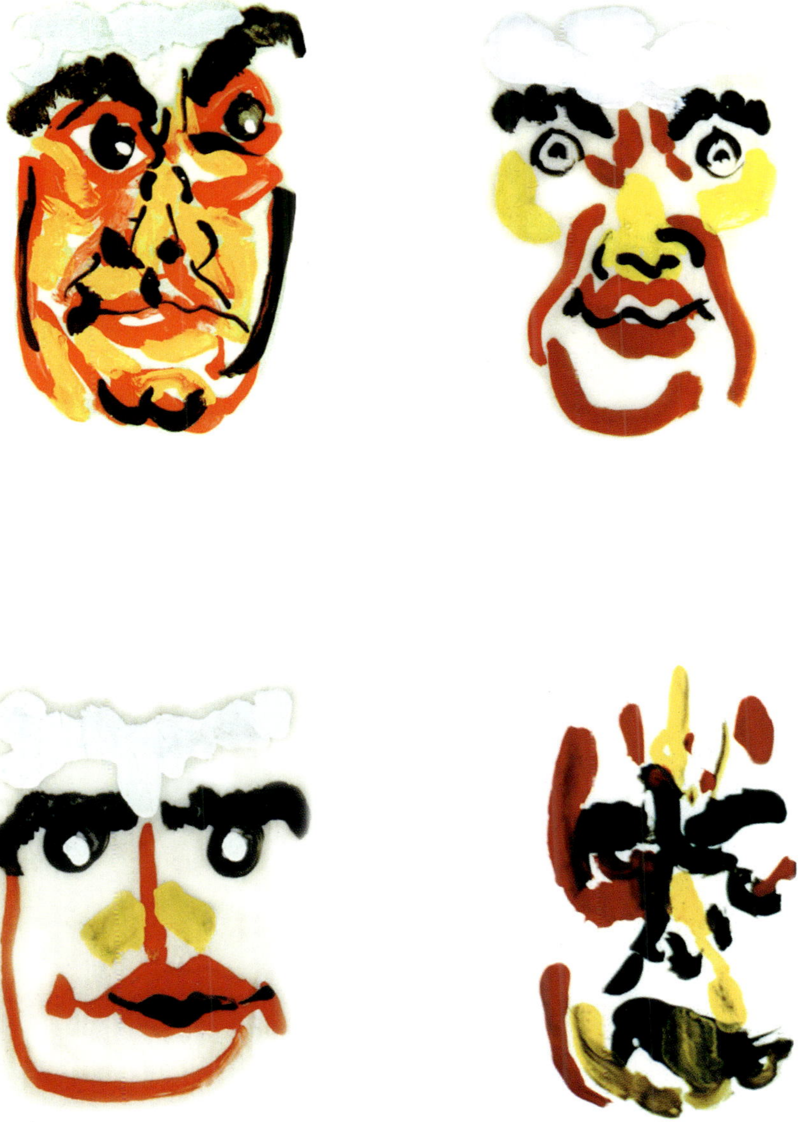

Four miniature self-portraits, 1984–1985
(reproduced larger than actual size).

# The "She" Paintings

Early in 1994, Adi Da indicated an intention to try media other than pen and ink wash for painting—media that would still allow the "immediacy and directness" of his method of relating to the subject.

After the new materials had been assembled, Adi Da was ready to begin. On the evening of March 30, 1994, in a single highly-energized event, he created thirty-five works which he later named "the 'She' Paintings". In a studio on his Fijian island-retreat, filled with moving female subjects, Adi Da intensively, and with great spontaneity, made each painting on paper while working at a large table. Painting with a circular "stirring" action, with the brush held far back on the handle, he once again worked without taking his eyes from the subject, not glancing down even when the paper was replaced for the next painting by an assistant.

Adi Da used a mélange of paint, oil-pastels, and oil-paint-sticks for each subject, with intentionally unconventional combinations of pure pigmented colors. He composed the paintings with energized brushstrokes, often forming geometric shapes. Large areas of white paper are left around each figure, also making geometric forms from the negative space. These aesthetic qualities, as well as the absence of one-point perspective, were all to re-emerge in the coming years as fundamental characteristics of Adi Da's art.

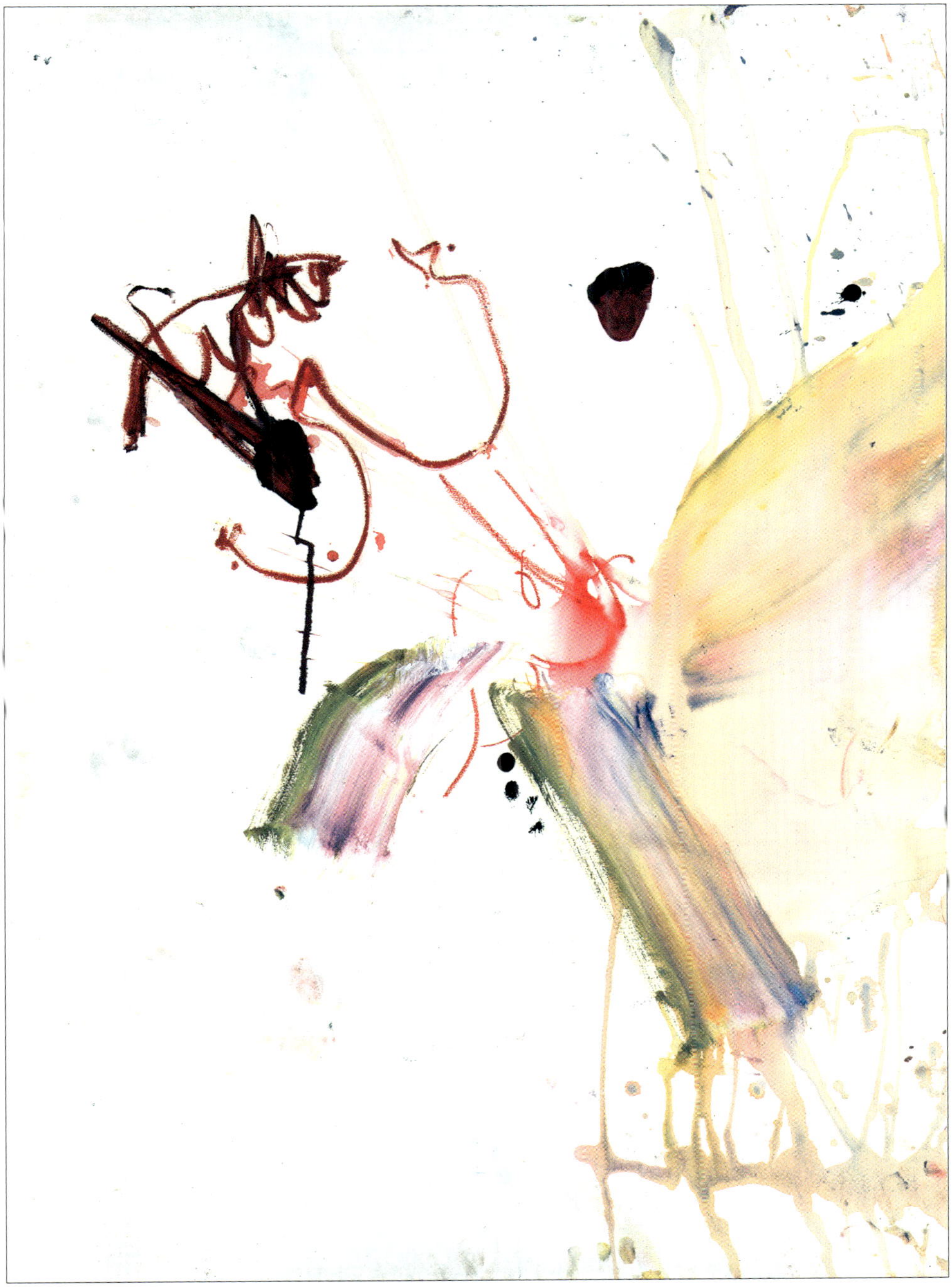

"She" Painting, 1994.
Liquid acrylic paint and oilbar on paper.

*The form of art I am talking about is one that takes place in the reality of feeling. The heart is the painter, so it is an ecstatic feeling in response to the totality of what is arising. Ecstatic—rather than ego-based. It is a process of feeling, rather than merely a process in concept or perception. It focuses on the total field of what is arising, rather than on the surface being painted. So the painted surface is not a reproduction of the process, but a reflection or an effect of it. The surface that is being painted is not glanced at much—it is felt. There is bodily awareness of it. Thus, it is controlled via the body, but it is not regarded via the eye or mind.*

*So the one making the art must be mindlessly occupied in feeling the total field perceived and the body works on the surface in such a manner to reflect that feeling-occupation with the total field. So it does not really make any difference what is in the field of the eye and the field of perception in any moment.*

Explaining why he chose to call these "the 'She' Paintings", Adi Da said:

*Men are angular. Women are spherical. If you paint women, you paint the whole universe. Every woman is a particularization of the one thing—the "She", the universal power.*

*A woman's body rotating expresses the unity of existence. It is all just "She".*

*A room without furnishing, and women rotating within it—this is the principal subject of painting.*

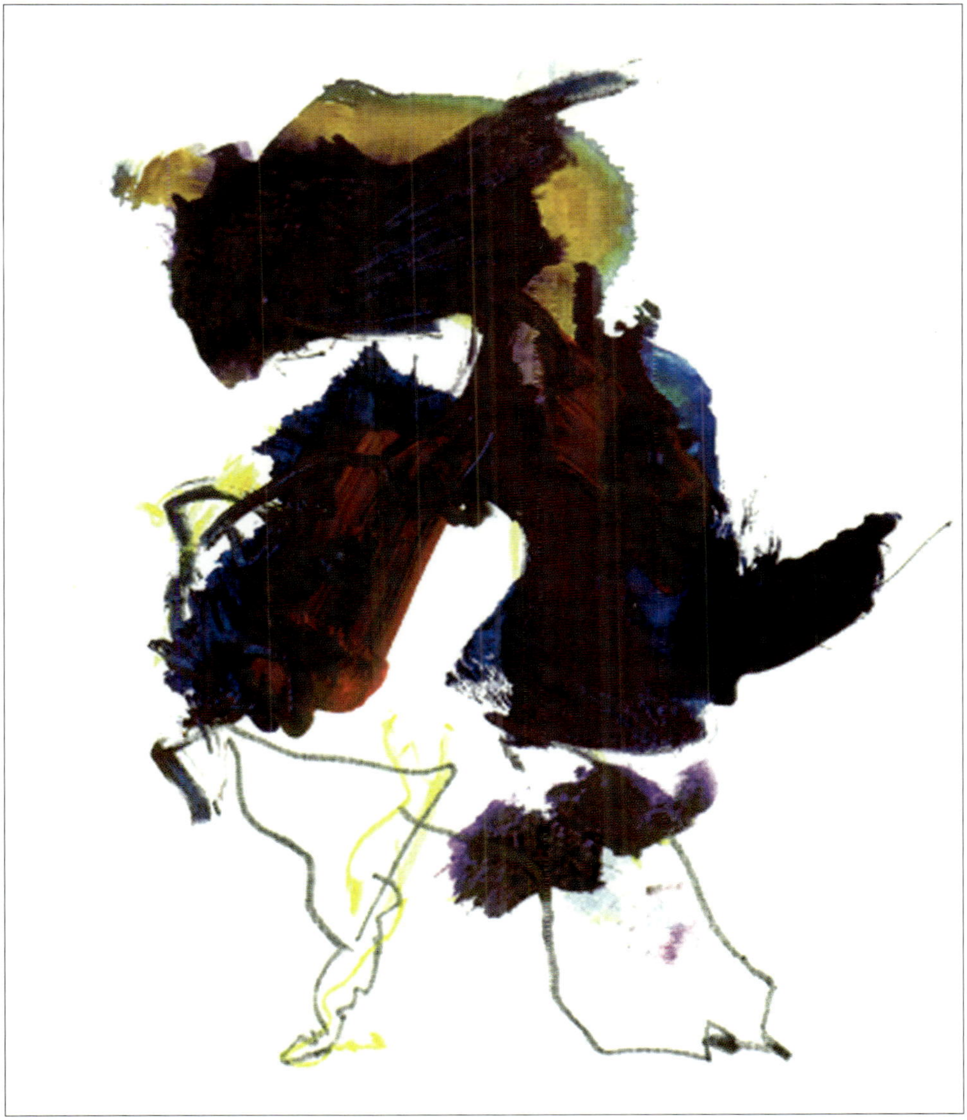

"She" Painting, 1994
Liquid acrylic paint and oilbar on paper.

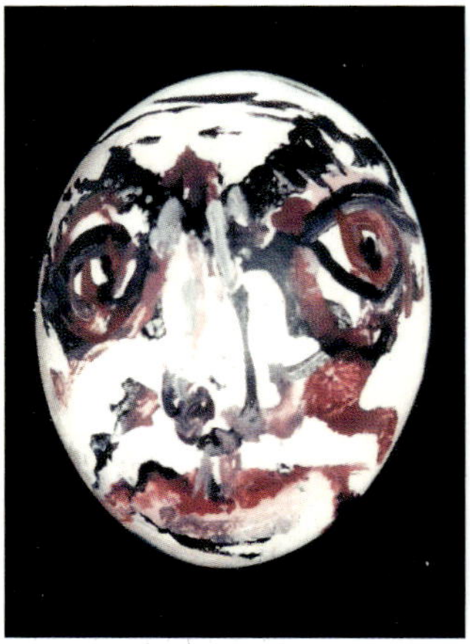

Egg portrait, 1996.
Acrylic paint.

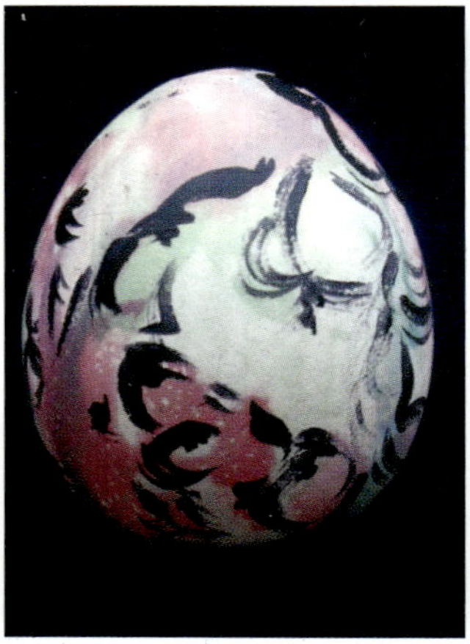

Egg (abstract), 1985.
Dye and acrylic paint.

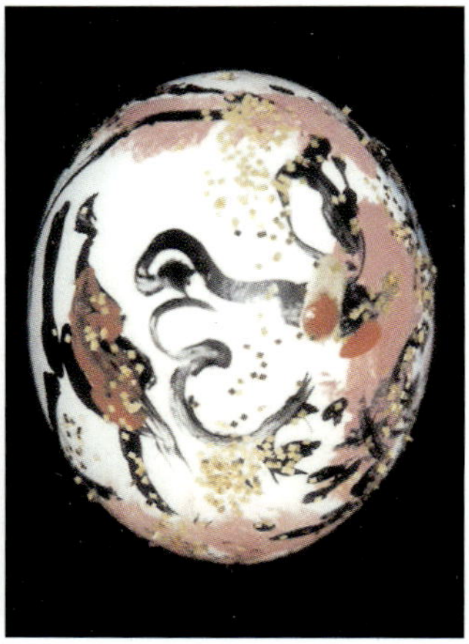

Egg portrait, 1996.
Acrylic paint and glitter.

## Eggs, Cookies, and Pumpkins

Taking traditional celebrations as occasions for serious artwork, Adi Da has used eggs, cookies, and even pumpkins as media for his abstract portraiture of reality. Dropping into deeply focused work during festive gatherings, Adi Da has in these moments extended his oeuvre to include new interpretations of familiar icons.

In his paintings on eggs, Adi Da often made a base of dyed color and then overlaid markers and paints. His work in cookies, some preserved in acrylic resin, includes icing portraits on dough "canvases". Adi Da's Halloween pumpkins are often sculptural assemblages, constructed at times with multiple vegetables, "wigs", and internal lighting and sound effects.

Adi Da's making art out of foodstuffs may be linked to the later appearance of eggs, fruits, and "dining" in his imagery—and even the phrase "the fruits of knowledge" in one of his suite titles. By working in these perishable, edible materials, Adi Da points to the fragility of life and the conditional realm as a place of constant sacrifice.

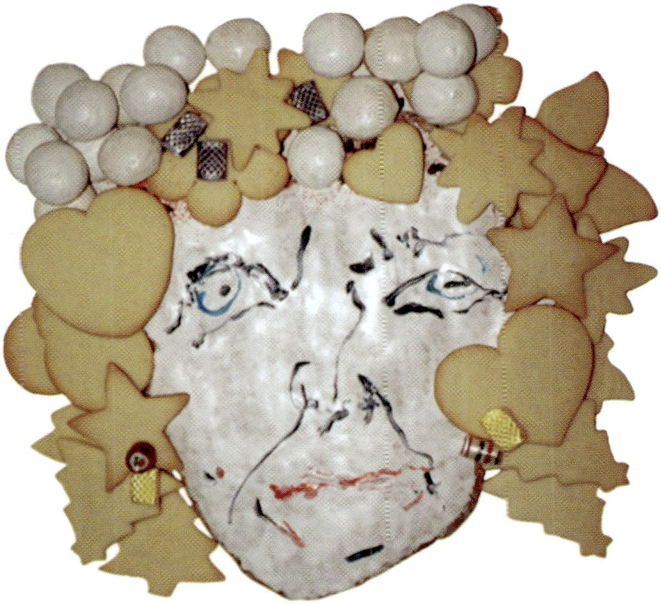

Portrait, 1995.
Cookie dough, icing, food coloring, hard candies.

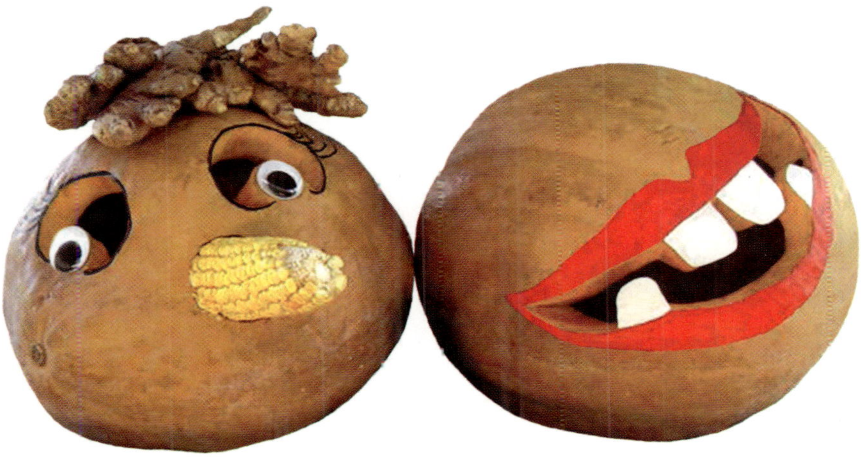

Pumpkin assembly, 2003.
Pumpkins, ginger, corncob, wiggle eyes, paint.

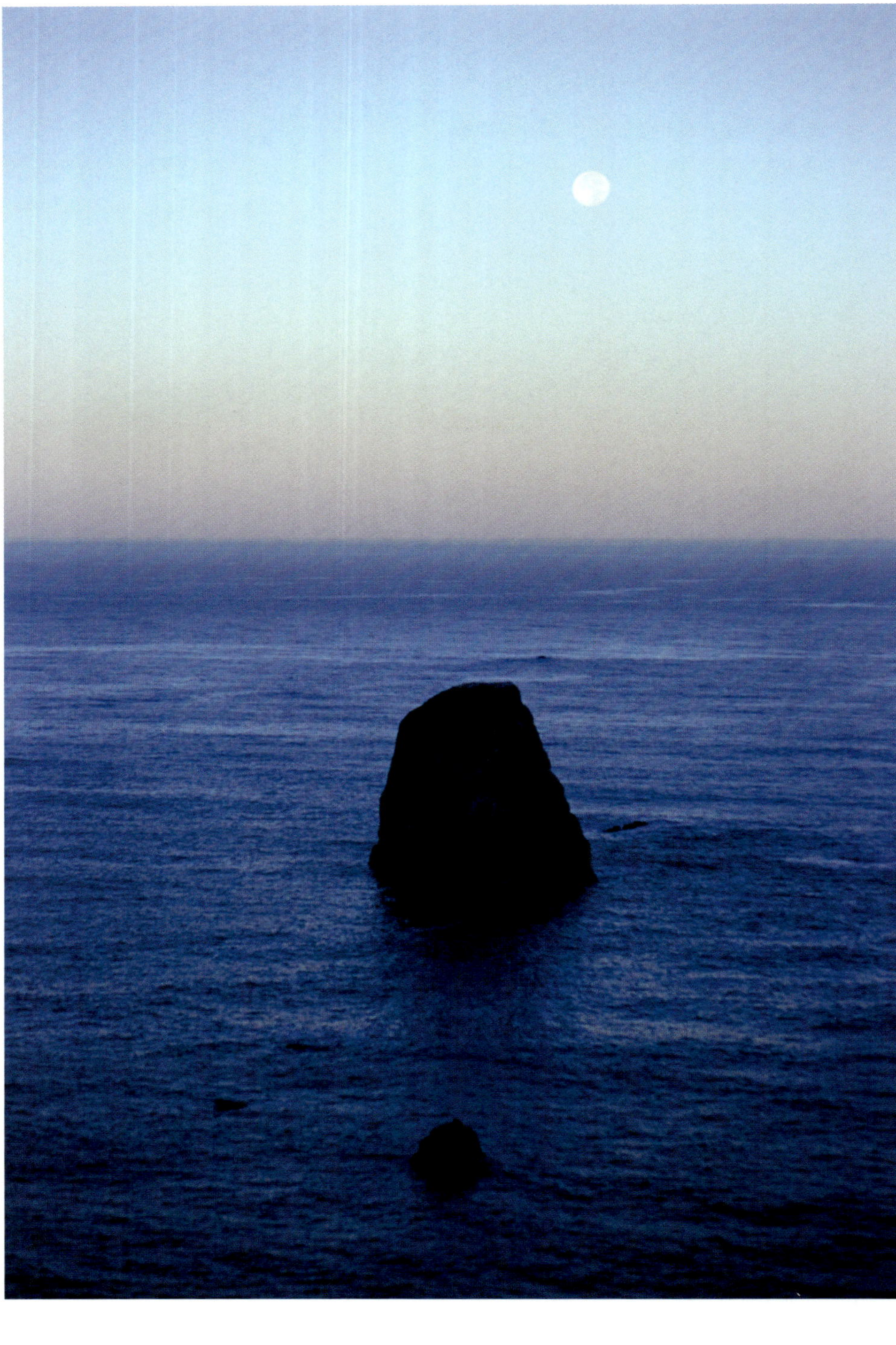

Tat Sundaram, 1998.

CHAPTER THREE

# Camera = "Point of View"

In late September 1998, Adi Da Samraj took up residence in a small house on the dramatic rocky coast of northern California. He was reminded of Tunitas (a beach where he lived during his Stanford years), and he named the house "Tat Sundaram", meaning "all of this is beautiful". Here, Adi Da used a camera for the first time in over two decades, capturing images of the moon setting over the huge monolithic rock in the sea just beside the house.

These photographs inaugurated an extraordinarily prolific period in Adi Da's art—resulting, within a few years' time, in tens of thousands of images. His choice of the camera as an artistic medium was a decisive breakthrough in his creation of an art that transcends "point of view". The technology itself became both the means and the metaphor for communicating a participation in reality free of the limitation of "point of view".

Soon after making these images of the moon, rock, and ocean, Adi Da announced he would make his "approach to photography" in three distinct phases: first choosing the equipment, then studying how to use it, and finally making pictures.

For the next six weeks, he researched every kind of camera equipment available, from 35mm to medium-format to large-format—six to eight hours a day—assessing each apparatus in great detail. One of his key criteria was that the equipment should not impede the fluidity of his physical movement. Most of all, the camera could not come between him and his response to the subject.

Between 1998 and 2004, Adi Da chose to use photography as the basis for his image-art. In 2006, he went on to combine photographs with the digital medium. However, whether created with the camera or with digital technology, he considers his images to be a form of "painting", using light itself as the primary medium of communication.

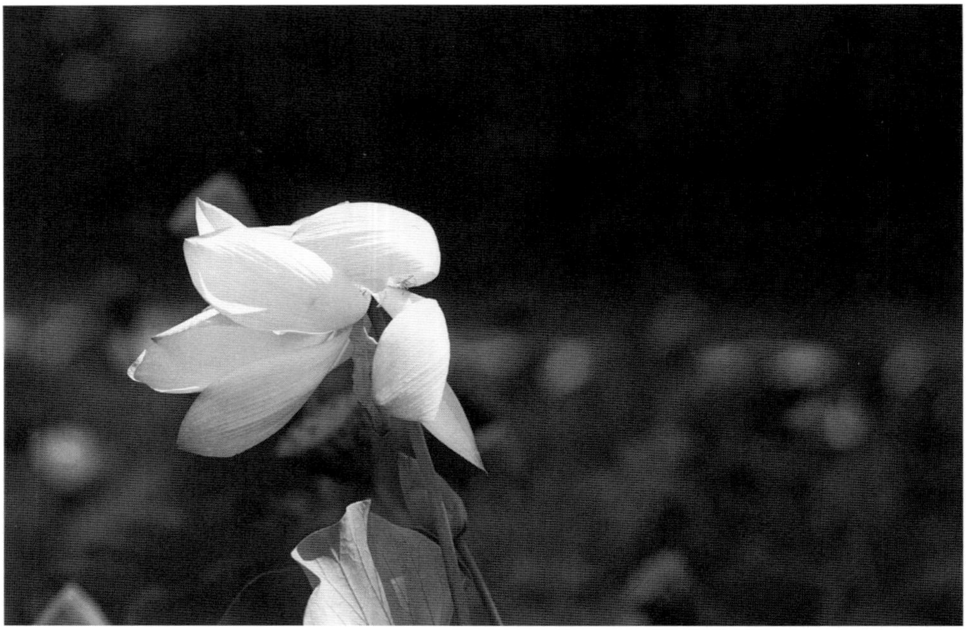

Kauai, 1999.

## Camera as Metaphor

As Adi Da combined himself more and more with photography as the primary tool for his artistry, he began to remark on the camera mechanism as a uniquely apt metaphor for the human body-mind—since both the camera and the human structure can be seen as viewing mechanisms with an interior means of recording what is viewed. In a 2001 essay entitled "Transcending the Camera: The Reality Beyond 'Point of View'", Adi Da speaks of this metaphor and also introduces his concept of the "room" as reality. Not coincidentally, "camera" is the Italian (and Latin) word for "room".

*The camera is "point of view" incarnate. The event of the camera registering an image on a piece of film replicates the human idea of what it is to see: The light of the "outside" world enters through a small aperture and is registered on a light-sensitive material. Thus, both the camera and the human being are mechanisms for registering reality from a particular "point of view" in space-time. The camera—like the human being—is a "point-of-view machine". Thus, the process of making photographs reflects the nature of the human event, of human experiencing.*

*The human individual in the midst of reality is like a camera in a room—perceiving everything from a fixed "point of view". But what does the room really look like? The room can be viewed from every possible "point of view" in space-time—not merely from any particular "point of view", or even a finite collection of "points of view". Therefore, no "point of view" can reveal the room, or reality itself, because every "point of view" is limited and essentially self-referring.*

*Reality itself always already exists. Reality itself is what exists prior to "point of view", before any individual "point of view" constructs its version of presumed "reality".*

*"Point of view" is the essence of ego-life: The apparently individual being presumes that he or she is a particularized "point", or organized "point of view", in space-time. And that "point" is "made" by contracting from the condition of totality—and, indeed, by contracting from even every mode, form, or condition of conditional existence. Therefore, the camera is a precise mechanical equivalent of the ego—because it, too, functions as fixed "point of view".*

*In my use of the camera, I work to make images that go beyond, and even undermine, the conventions of "point of view". Such images transcend the limitation that would seem to be inherent in the photographic mechanism (or "'point-of-view' machine"). They allow the viewer to see and feel the "room"—or the world, or reality—as it is, beyond the ego's self-reference. And such images thereby become a non-verbal means of "picturing" the essential human process of transcending the ego—going beyond the fixed "point of view" of the ego, or the core presumption of separateness.**

## Stretching the Limits of the Camera

Once Adi Da Samraj started shooting, he quickly began exploring the potentials of the camera as an artistic mechanism. In addition to creating photographs in the "classic" manner (such as the lotus photograph on the facing page), he systematically investigated the possibilities of creating non-ordinary views of the world—through overexposure, long exposures, foreshortening, and the blurring of focus. In so doing, he was building a visual vocabulary by which he could more and more fully express that the ordinary "ego's-eye" view of the world does not represent all of reality.

Although Adi Da's initial photographs taken in October 1998 were in color, he soon chose to work only in black-and-white. It was more than three years before he once again worked in color.

*Published in *The* Quandra Loka *Suite: 52 Views* (West Hollywood, CA: Louis Stern Fine Arts, 2003), p. 13.

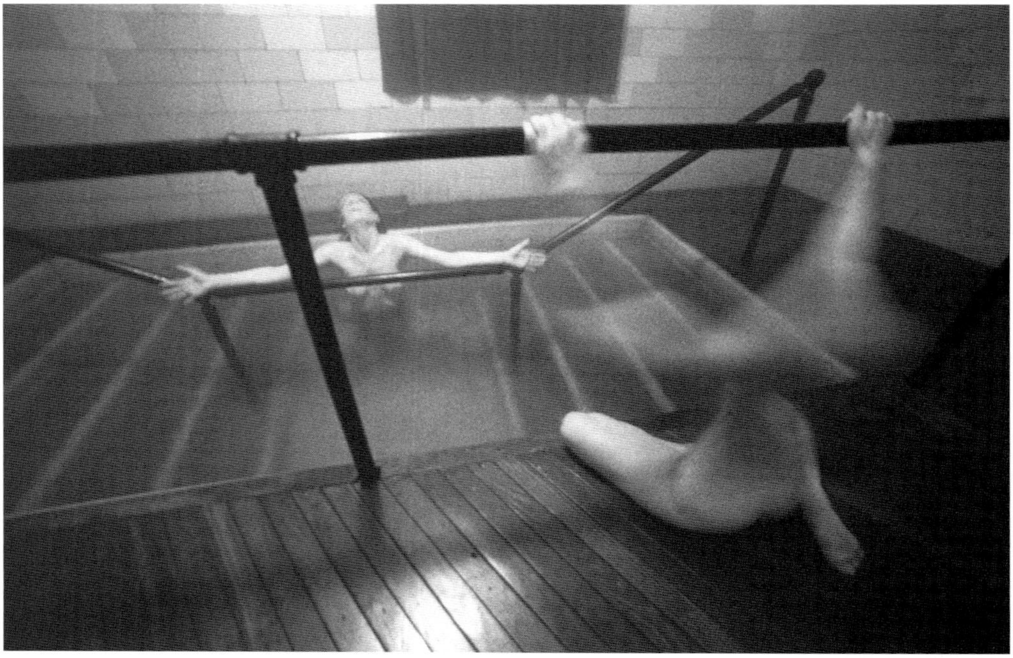

The Mountain Of Attention Sanctuary,
Northern California, 1999.

## "Painting" the Redwoods

One day in June 2000, as he was walking through a northern California redwood forest, Adi Da began speaking of a desire to go beyond the kinds of images he had already made—and to go even further beyond the "point of view" inherent in the camera itself. Having said this, he suddenly started manipulating the exposure time, the lens aperture, and the camera body itself very freely.

The new images were striations-in-light, in-motion and beyond conventional realism. Adi Da had initiated what he referred to as "free light-imagery". He acknowledged that, in these very painterly photographic images, he had found a way of making "photographs that are the tangible manifestation of a different mode of experience".

Soon after this breakthrough, Adi Da began to make intensive use of the capacity of an automated camera to record multiple exposures on a single frame of film. Very quickly, in-camera multiple exposure was to become his principal means for creating images that literally go beyond any single fixed "point of view".

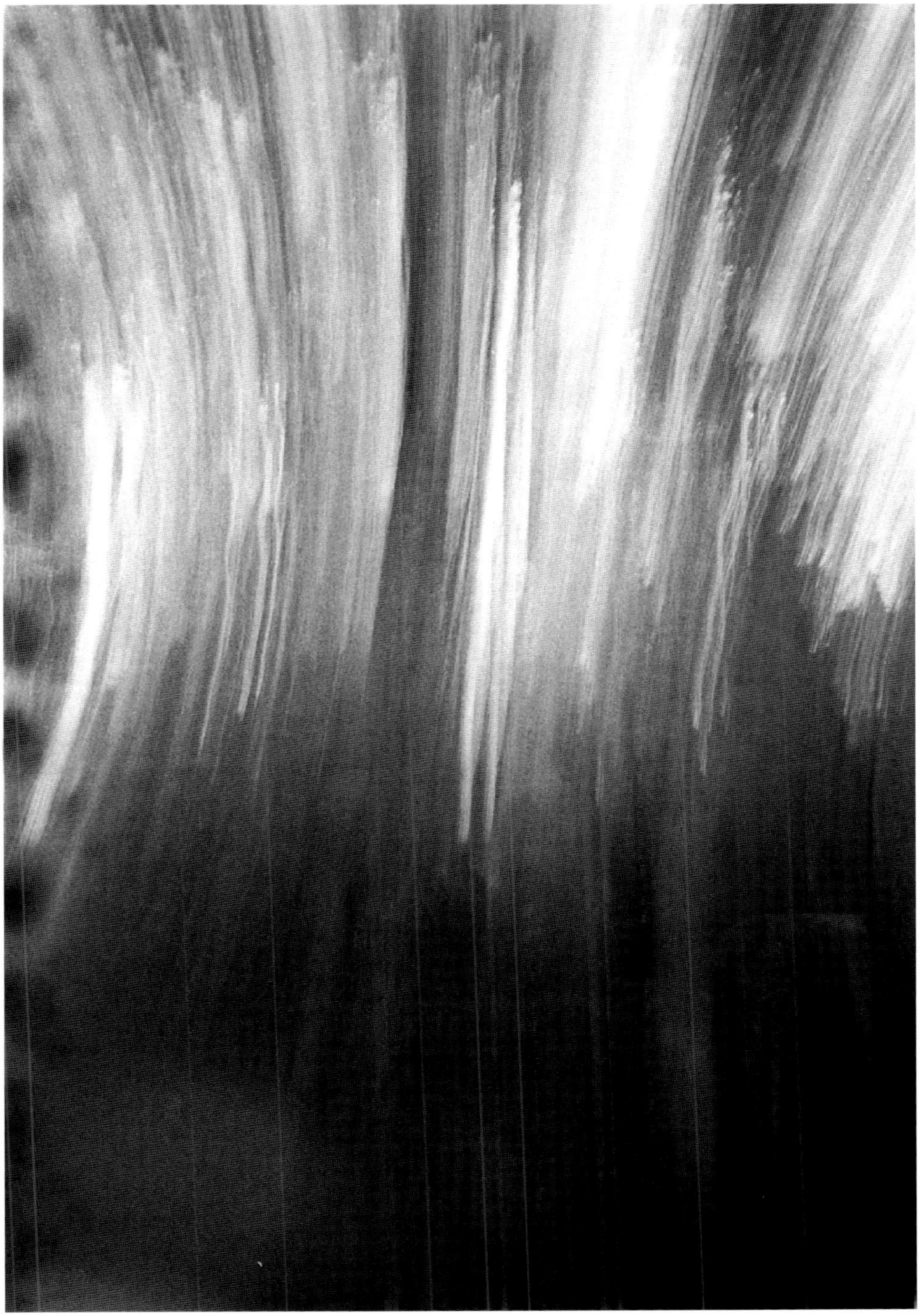

Northern California, 2000.

CHAPTER FOUR

# Simultaneous Views: Multiple Exposure

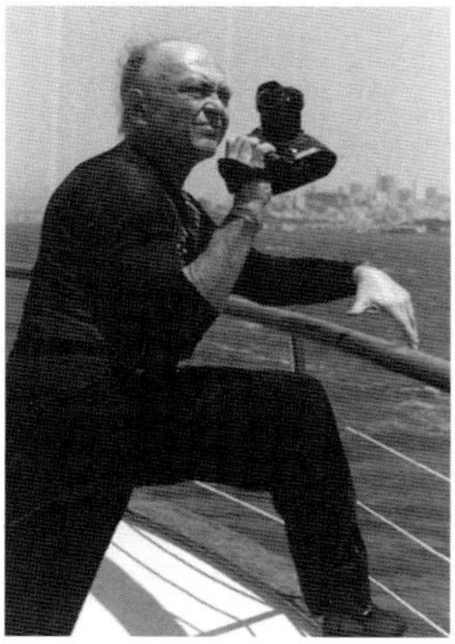

On a late summer day in August of 2000, Adi Da made a series of photographs while taking a cruise in the San Francisco Bay. As the boat passed under the Golden Gate Bridge, and then back again, Adi Da created a series of images of the boat, the bridge, and those accompanying him on board. This group of images, *Through the Gate*, marks the genesis of two highly significant developments in Adi Da's oeuvre: his first use of multiple exposure on film and, also, his organization of images into suites.

The abstraction of multiple exposure became a new means for Adi Da to draw the viewer beyond "point of view". Within a suite, Adi Da would often place a non-multiple view of a subject, recognizable as person or thing, at the beginning of a sequence of images, followed by images with progressively more and more layers of exposures from all angles. An identifiable person or thing thereby "turned into" an abstract vision of light.

Adi Da's commentary on his art from this period echoes his critique of modernist abstraction of thirty years prior:

*If reality is reduced to a shattered abstraction without meaning, then the beautiful is no longer there, the beloved is no longer there. I use the photographic medium precisely because it inherently reflects human and conditional reality and form.*

*The visual abstraction in these images is not something separate or separative, but an expression of the seamlessness of reality. I work to move the viewer into ecstasy—abstracted beyond the ego's modes of perception. Ecstasy abstracts absolutely (but not meaninglessly)—beyond all presumed "difference" of "self" and "other".*

*Through the Gate*, 2000.
Single Image.

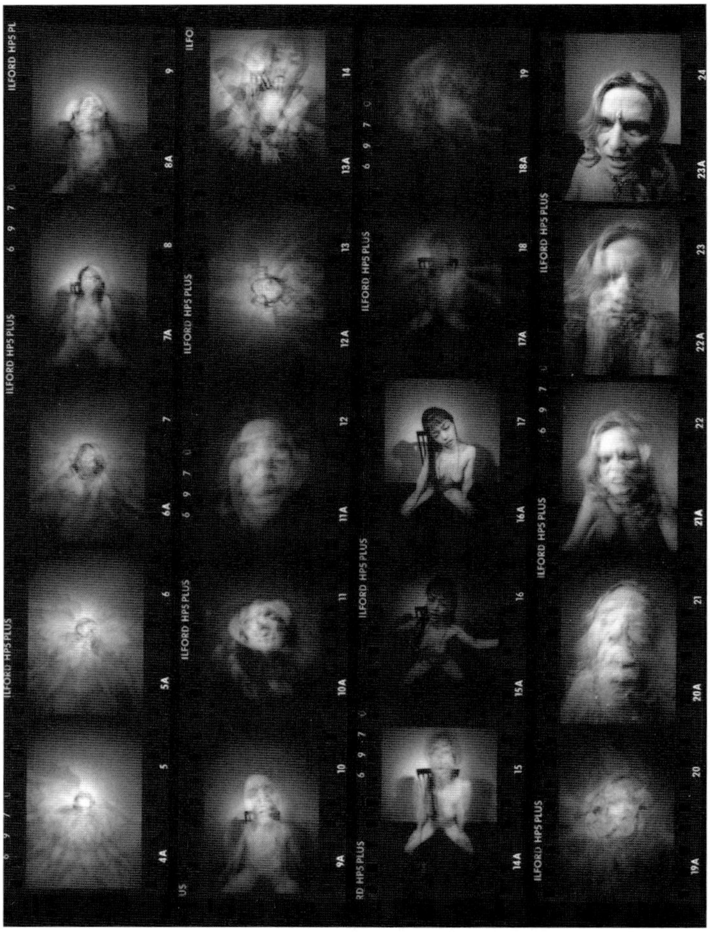


Contact sheet for *The Aaarghh Suite* (detail).

For those familiar with the rigors of the photographic process, Adi Da's multiple-exposure work is a remarkable demonstration of his technical and aesthetic mastery—and of his extraordinary capacity for visual memory and precision. To layer up to ten exposures in a single frame required the utmost concentration and steadiness as he composed each image in-camera—retaining all of the superimposed images in his "mind's eye", while simultaneously measuring the lighting by eye. Adi Da made this body of work without any digital manipulation of images, using traditional darkroom technology only. As a further challenge, Adi Da often worked with freely moving subjects—or, as in his first suite, even on a moving boat. The contact sheets of the rolls from this period are a testament to this unique dimension of Adi Da's work.

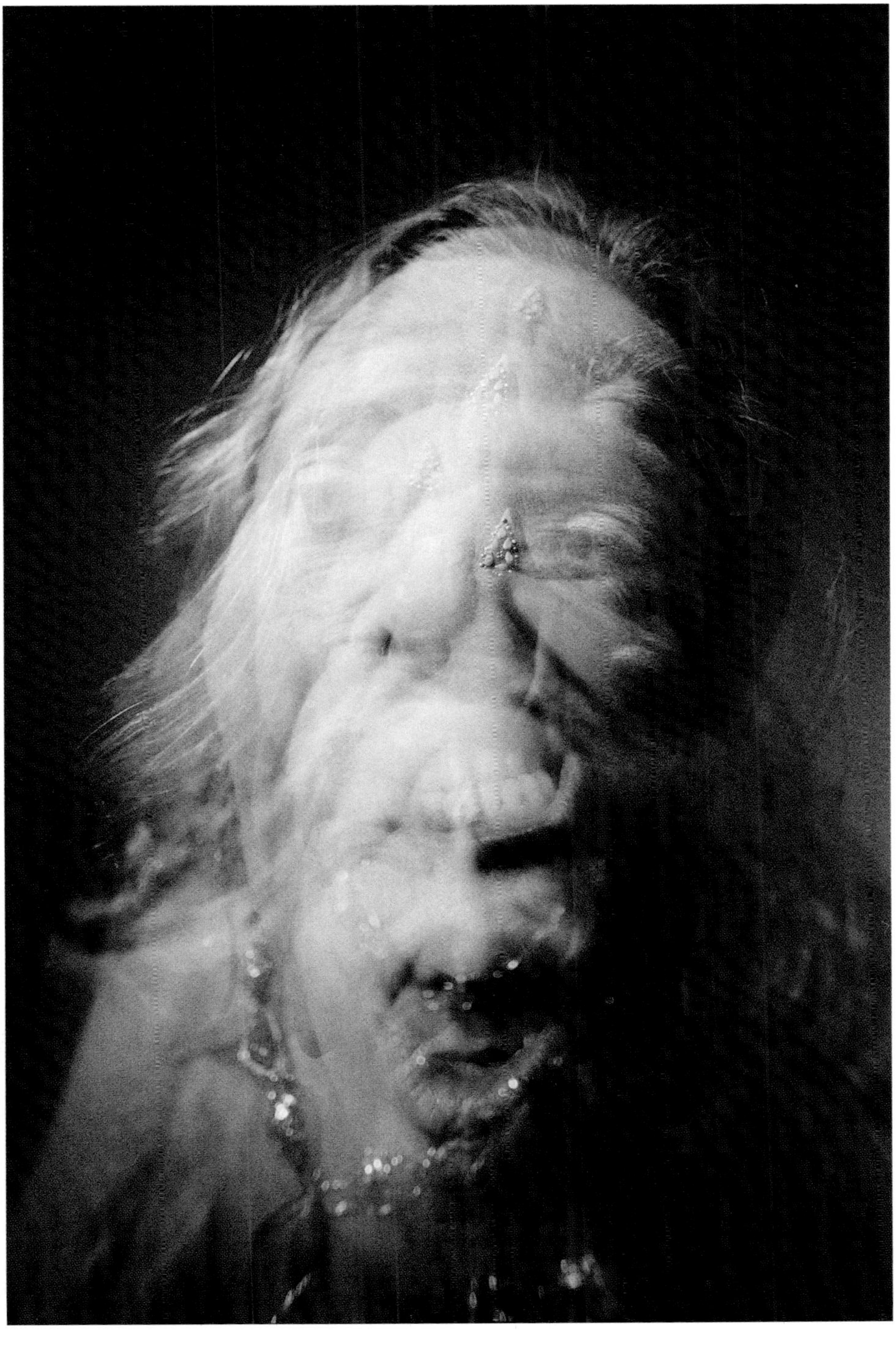

*The Aaarghh Suite*, 2001.
Single Image.

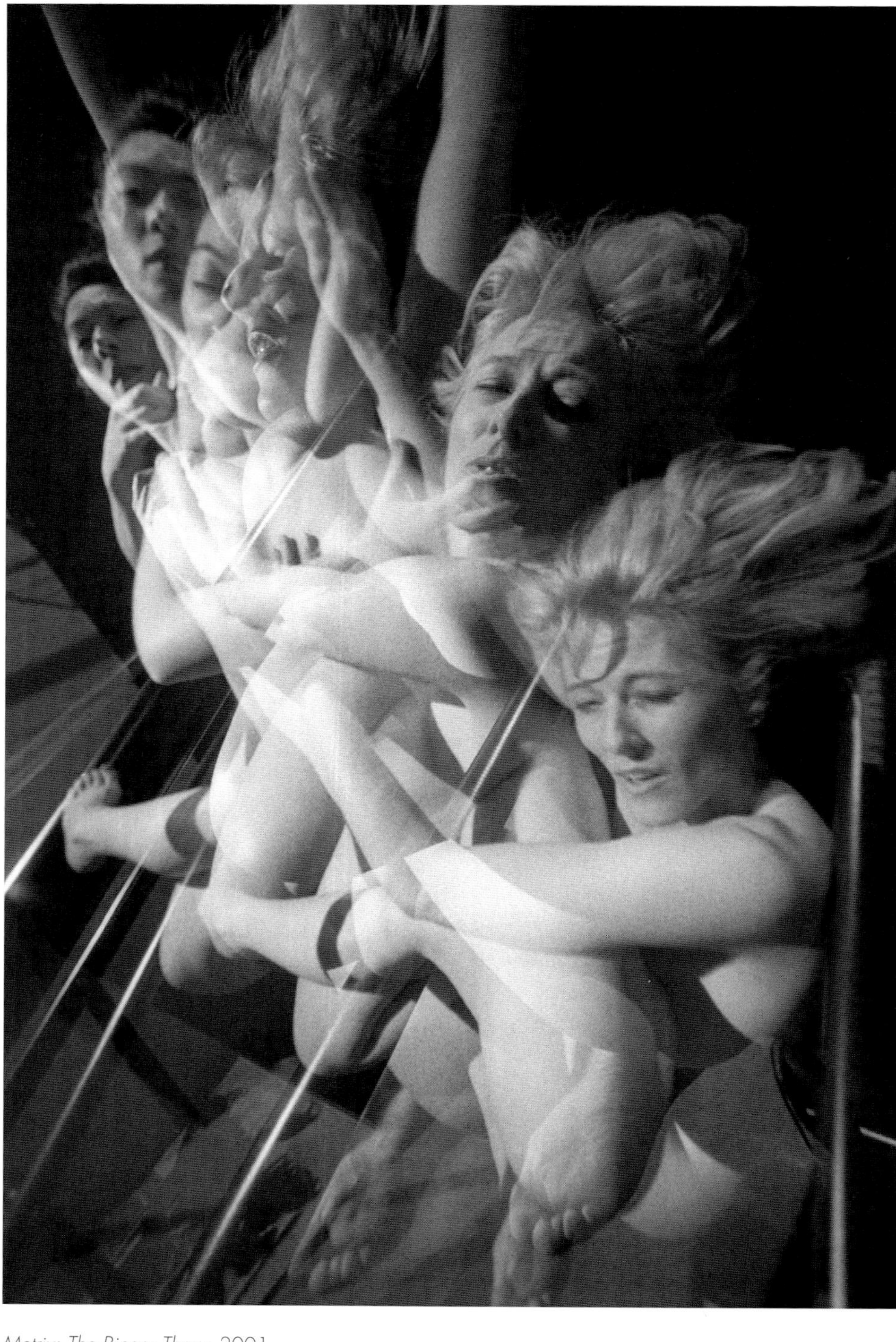

*Metrix: The Binary Thaw*, 2001.
Single Image.

## Adi Da and Cubism

"Point of view" has a well-known history in visual art—from the development of perspective in the Renaissance to the Cubists' mode of presenting more than one "point of view" at once within a painting. Adi Da's presentation of multiple "points of view", however, is about what is beyond "point of view", or without "point of view" at all. He distinguishes his images from the pivotal work of Cézanne and the Cubists—with respect to the intention of his work, as well as how it is made.

*In early modernist art, such as the work of Cézanne or of Cubists such as Picasso and Braque, images were made based on moving the "point of view" around, as if the artist, in moving about while looking at the subject, made each element of the image based on being in a different position relative to the subject. So you would see an image made as if it had many elements, each of which were seen from a different "point of view".*

*My image-art is about the transcending of "point of view" itself. It is not about many "points of view", but about no "point of view". It is not about either the representation or the non-representation of "objects". It is about what is inherently non-"objective".*

*This is a way of making images that is beyond both modernism and post-modernism. This way of making images is about the inherent transcending of "point of view", about art that is not about "point of view", not imitating how things look from a "point of view", or even many "points of view". It is about no "point of view", and inherently non-"objective" reality.*

CHAPTER FIVE

# Successive Views: Suites in Space and Time

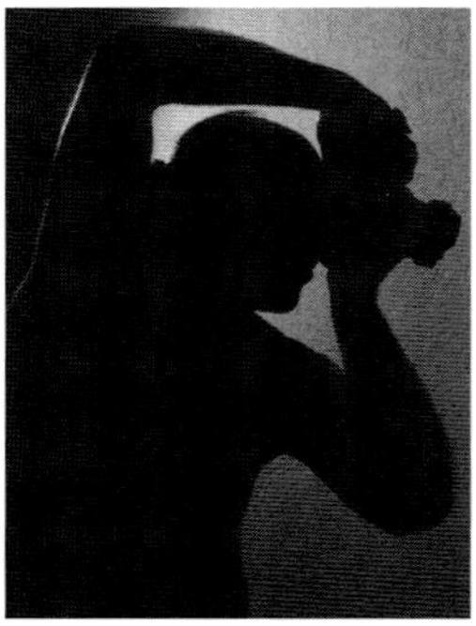

Adi Da's work with suites of multiply layered images marked an unprecedented outpouring of his creativity. He expanded his palette of outdoor subjects in late 2000 with expeditions into Yosemite in winter snows, more work with the monolithic rock of Tat Sundaram, and the cityscapes of San Francisco. Then, in February 2001, Adi Da Samraj suddenly established his first indoor set—a simple white-walled room at the Mountain Of Attention retreat sanctuary in northern California. His intention was to work with the nude figure—"the unclothed and, therefore, non-social personality"—and to deal, both artistically and spiritually, with "fundamental issues of existence". With a small group of photographic subjects he had known for many years, Adi Da began a non-stop process of photographic shooting and breakspeed innovation. An intensive nightly cycle—shooting up to six rolls, or over two hundred frames, reviewing his images by dawn, and sequencing the new images the next day—became his constant process for nearly three months. As part of this remarkable aesthetic process, he composed suites using every frame he shot, with no image discarded.

As Adi Da worked on the set, his concentration on every element of the space, his attention for his photographic subjects, and his touch of the equipment were a performance of great sensitivity and freedom. The images reveal Adi Da's vision of the "room" and the beings within it as a seamless realm of light, a transformative space. The multiple-exposed images, sequenced into suites, were Adi Da's depiction of the "room" from beyond any single "point of view". Instead of attempting to capture single shots as if time could be frozen into fixed moments, Adi Da showed each "view" of space-in-time as a continuous circle of experience, to be seen from any point at any moment.

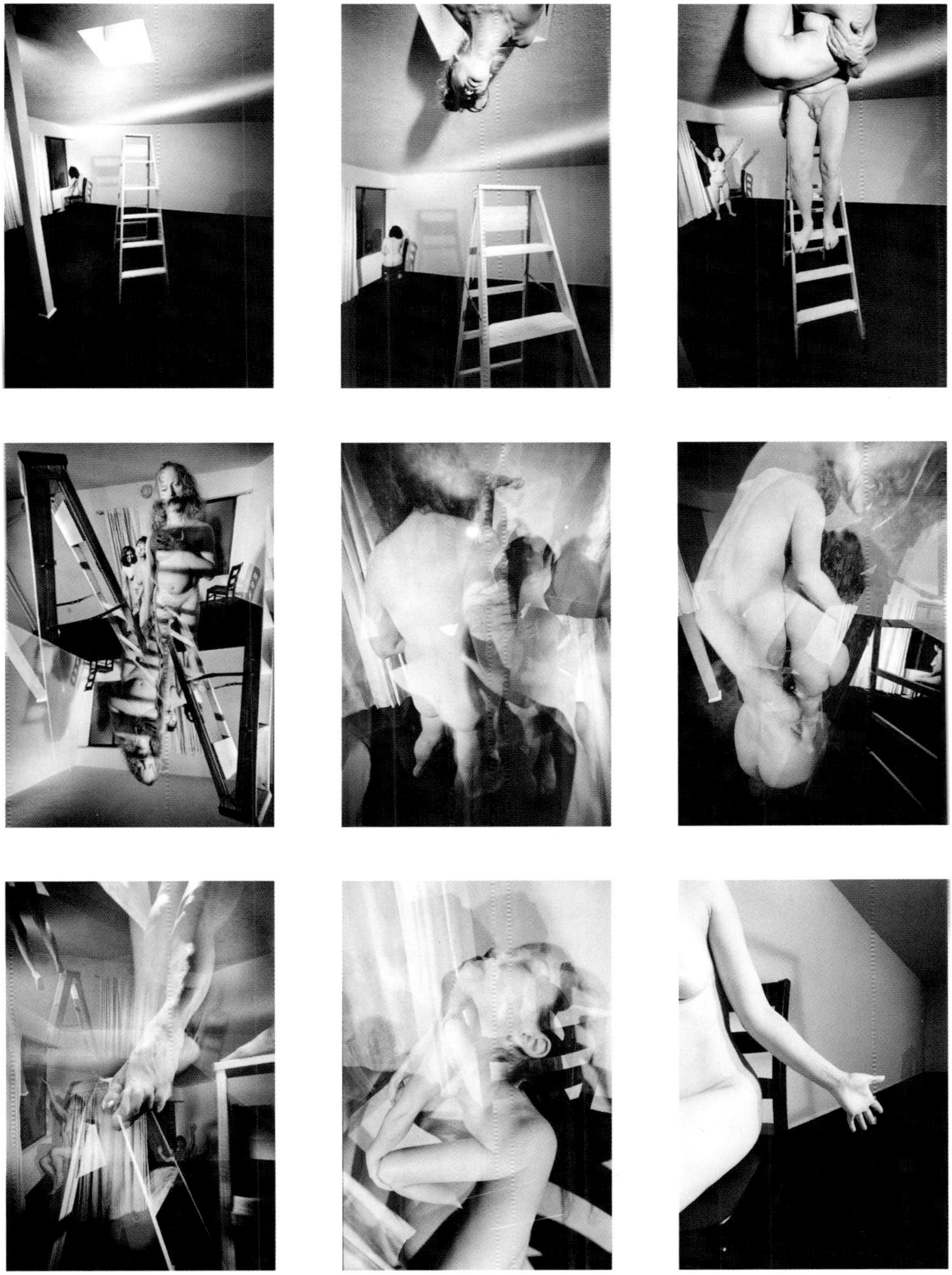

*The Virgin Suite*, 2001.
Nine Images.

## The "Language" of the "Room"

As the suites developed and expanded at an incredible pace over this time, so did Adi Da's work with archetypes and his development of a unique language of meaning. For example, a single classically proportioned black chair—and later, its exact duplicate in white—became Adi Da's symbol for the "seat of consciousness". One night, he decided to make a square hole that already existed in the ceiling into a key element of the set. Inserting a light to shine down from within the opening, Adi Da soon referred to it as "the hole in the universe". With this new element, the set also corresponded to his metaphor of the camera-as-room, the hole representing the aperture. This basic set became Adi Da's communication of "the room of mind"—the place of both illusion (within the room) and potential illumination (from "above").

Adi Da initiated the new ceiling hole in his narrative masterpiece, *The Virgin Suite (An Inexhaustible Supply of Virgins): To Accompany The Iconic Procession of Mother, Daughter, and Male Other in the Room of Mind*, in which a young woman was lowered through the opening, in a "birth" into the room, and the mother then ascends back into the opening. Here, the ladder symbolizes the mythical archetype of "ascension to heaven", and even the human subjects become archetypes of meaning.

## *Fun House*

Adi Da's work on his first indoor set culminated with his epic suite *Fun House (The Spherical Skirt): An Indefinitely Unfolding Procession of Iconic Imagery—for He, She, and the Only Horse in the Wild*. For this suite, the room came to life with a collection of artifacts from the Coney Island amusement park in New York. Most prominent was a larger-than-life mechanical laughing woman from the entrance to the old fun house—a place Adi Da had visited many times as a child. Placing her in the set with great intention, as if installing the deity of a temple, Adi Da named her "the Laughing Mama". The rest of the remarkable collection included a massive cast-metal mule (weighing over a ton) that had once kicked when the target on its rump was hit by a ball, large ominous clown faces, and the splintering letters of the original FUN HOUSE signage. The fact that these were actual "pieces" of Coney Island, with which Adi Da had come into contact as a boy, signaled their importance to him as autobiographical yet universal icons.

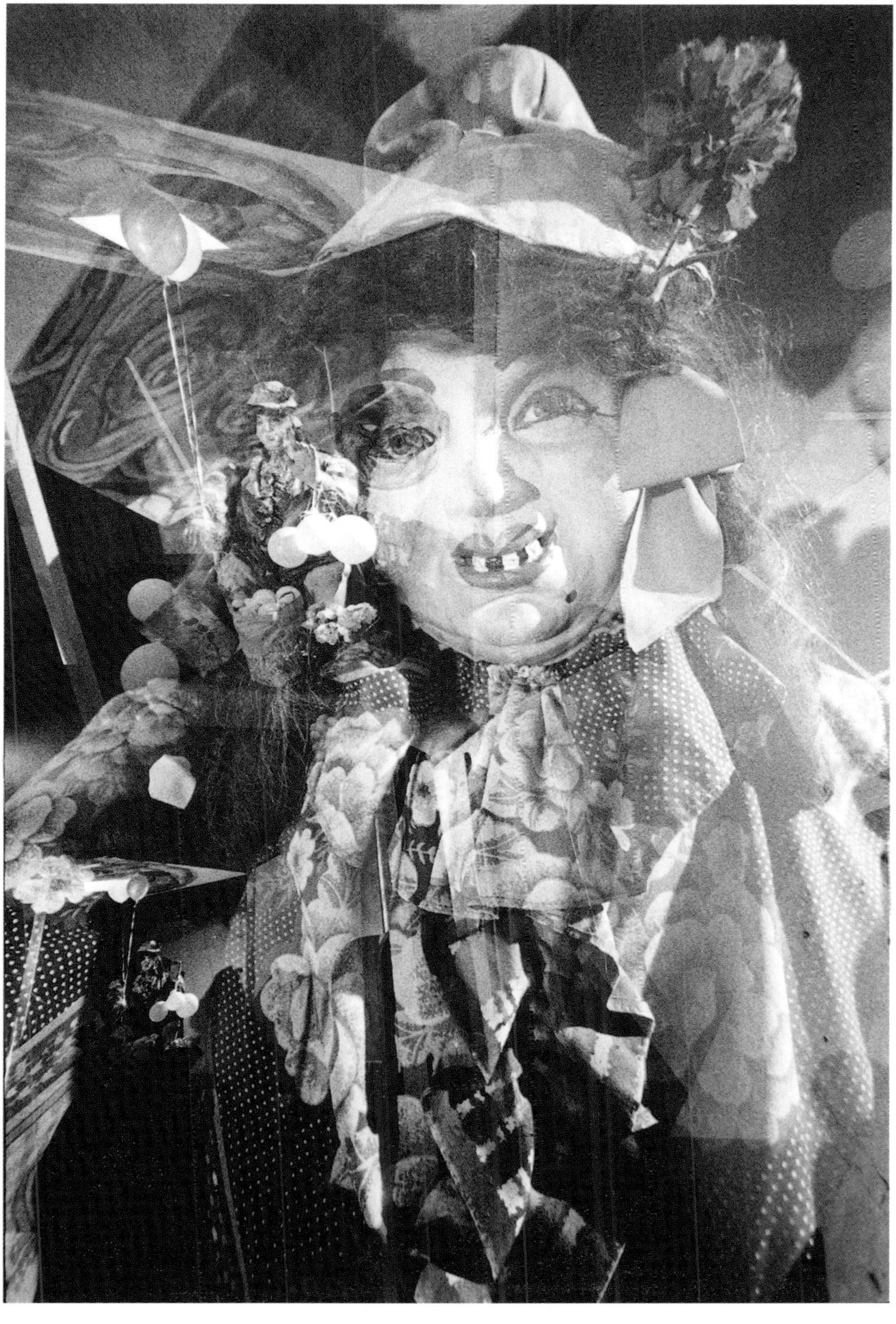

*Fun House*, 2001.
Single Image.

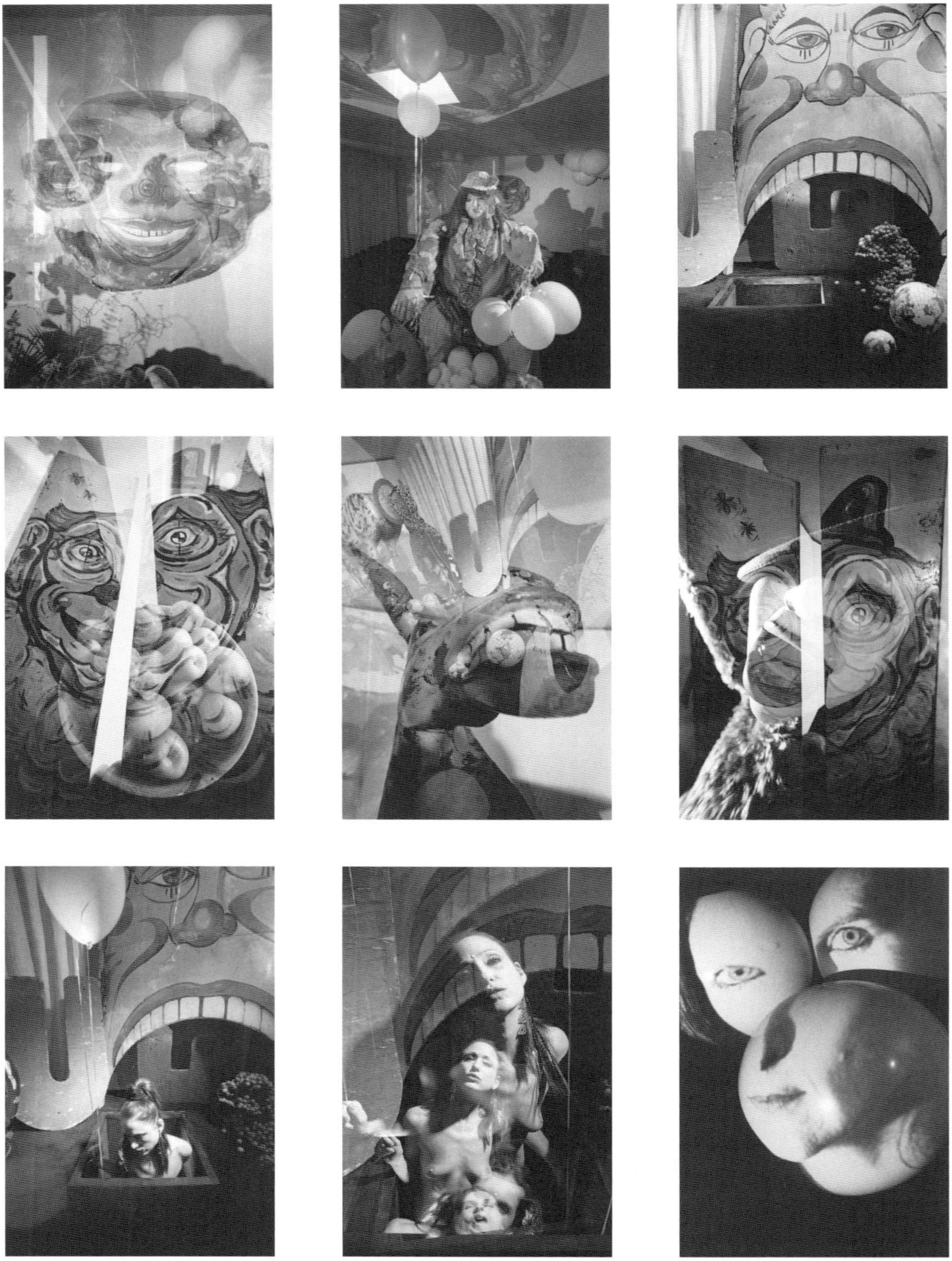

*Fun House*, 2001.
Nine Images.

As Adi Da explained, this bizarre setting was his "map" of the body, "the archetype of human space". The two holes—one in the ceiling and now another one added in the floor—represented the entrance into bodily life (floor hole) and the departure from it (ceiling hole). The Laughing Mama, he said, was the embodiment of a universe indifferent to mortality, cackling madly as you fall into the "pit" of death. But she also, paradoxically, if you notice, points you to the radiant ceiling hole and source of light.

While making *Fun House*, Adi Da spoke of the necessity for a serious approach to life, and how his images can aid that process.

*You are nothing more than a balloon caught between an indefinable, real, bright-lighted lady at one end of the "room" and a fathomless, cold, dark "something" at the other end. A tenuous balance—and no way to survive anyway. You only have that instant between the two holes to "get it". Until the balloon pops, you have just that much opportunity. So that means life is a very serious matter.*

Fun House *is about what controls—and, in some sense, even owns—your life. It is profound, and terrible, and great, and beautiful—all these things. The images of* Fun House *are made to assist you in truly encountering and really feeling the nature of everything that is conveyed in these images.*

## Love's Point Renewed

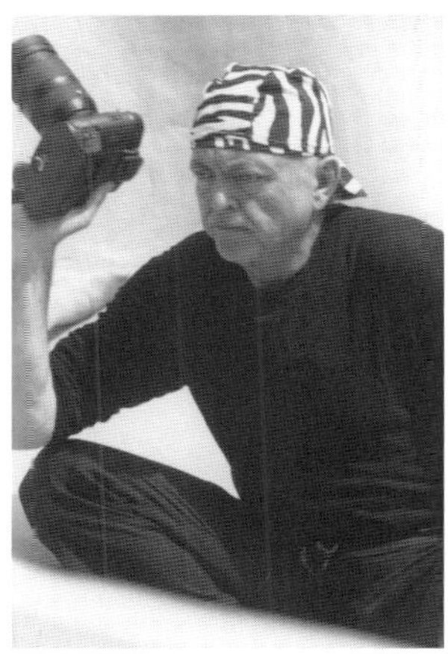

After *Fun House*, Adi Da resided for a time in a house not far from the Mountain Of Attention, situated on a precipice high above Clear Lake, the largest natural lake within California. Soon, in the bright summer solstice sunlight, Adi Da was moved to do outdoor photographic work for the first time in months. *Love's Point Renewed* was a burst of beauty, images combining the female form with flowers and plants, sky and lake views, and an innovative element: painted fabrics. He indicated the significance of this new suite with a humorous remark: "There is life after *Fun House*."

Every day, over a ten-day period, Adi Da would start shooting in the afternoon, when the blazing sun was at its peak, enduring temperatures into the hundreds while he exerted himself to new heights of artistry. When the suite was first presented, in a screening at the Mountain Of Attention, Adi Da composed a poem to accompany it.

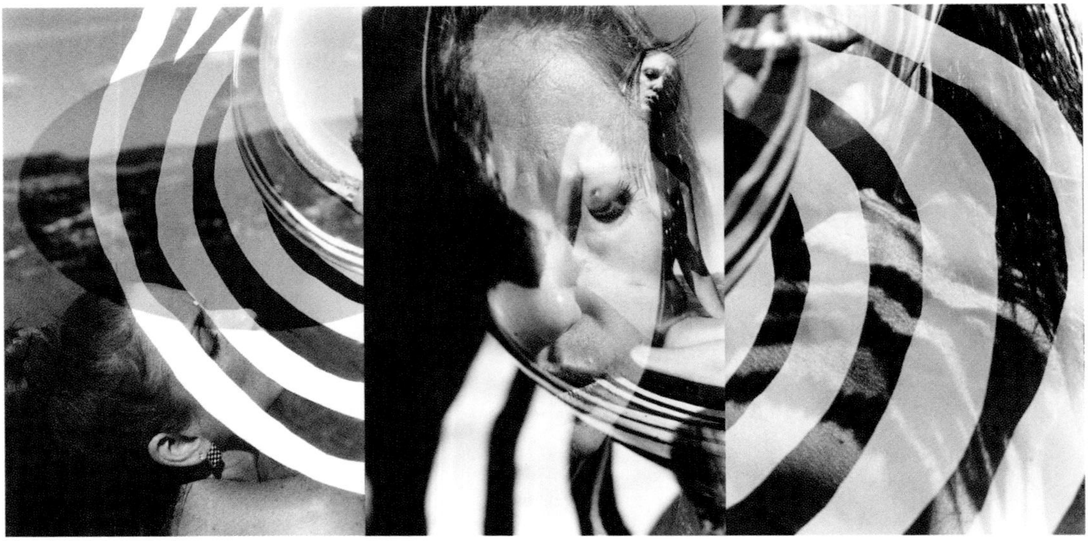

*Love's Point Renewed*, 2001.
Triptych.

Love Comes To Here In Time,
and Numbers All the Things
of Beauty In the House.
A Single Room Is Shown To Be
—A Unity, Within and Every Where.
No Point of View Is Stood Apart.
No Word Is Made To Say,
This Space Is Empty,
or, This Place Is Full.
Only Light Itself Is Come
—A Merest Touch of Brightness
Neither Mind Nor Body Can Deny.
It Is the Heart's Explanation of Reality.
It Is Reality, Plain Spoken To the Heart
—and By the Heart Alone.
It Is the Beautiful, Itself.

## ADI DA SAMRAJ: BLACK-AND-WHITE SUITES

August 2000–June 2001

*Through the Gate*. 53 Images.

*City Light*. 52 Images.

*Tat Sundaram (This Is That Which Is Beautiful)*. 139 Images.

*The First Yosemite Suite*. 353 Images.

*Sisters*. 13 Images.

*Four Women*. 59 Images.

*The Burden of Two*. 7 Images.

*The Cult of Pairs*. 27 Images.

*Two Many*. 49 Images.

*The Seat of The Passions*. 31 Images.

*Mother and Daughter*. 45 Images.

*Brahma, Vishnu, and Forsythe*. 16 Images.

*The Aaarghh Suite*. 27 Images.

*Tripura's Seat*. 45 Images.

*Five Men*. 20 Images.

*The Re-Assertion of Perfume in the Instant of Time (Images In Solo and Duo—A Pair Each)*. 114 Images.

*She Overhead (The Small Sequence)*. 8 Images.

*Repeatedly New*. 26 Images.

*The Wedding Album*. 21 Images.

*The Virgin Suite (An Inexhaustible Supply of Virgins): To Accompany the Iconic Procession of Mother, Daughter, and Male Other in the Room of Mind*. 144 Images.

*The Mere Event (Of Mir and Daily News)*. 54 Images.

*Metrix (The Binary Thaw)*. 142 Images.

*The Eternal Vigil of Monumental Art*. 38 Images.

*The Analog of Flora Mata (Two Roses Touched by the First Visible Idea of Reality)*. 168 Images.

*The Re-Birth of the Idea of Oranges*. 45 Images.

*21 (Exactly)*. 36 Images.

*Fun House (The Spherical Skirt): An Indefinitely Unfolding Procession of Iconic Imagery—for He, She, and the Only Horse in the Wild*. 658 Images.

*Open Water*. 104 Images.

*Love's Point Renewed*. 297 Images.

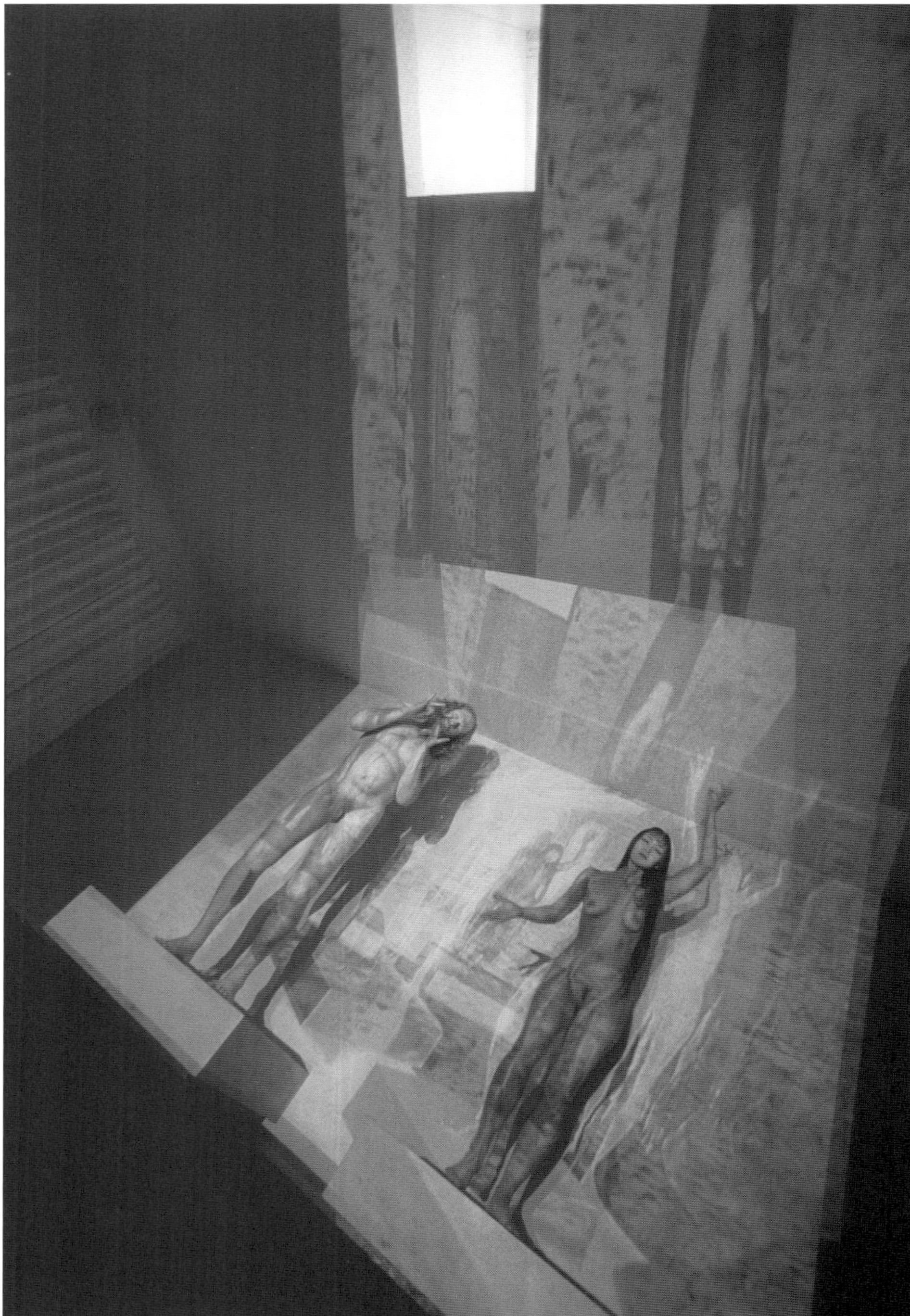

*The Eternal Vigil of Monumental Art*, 2001.
Single Image.

CHAPTER SIX

# Moving Views: Video Suites and Stills

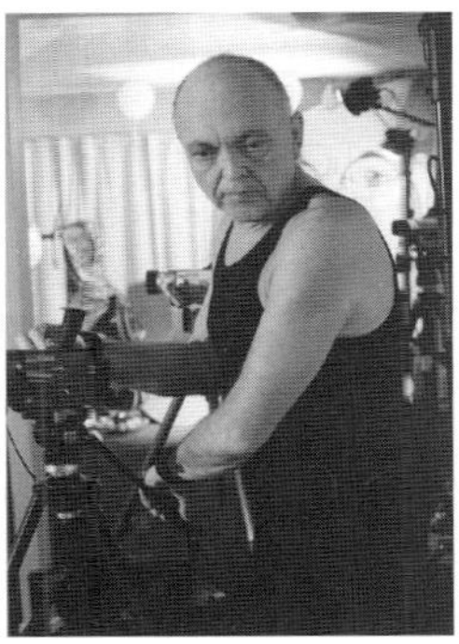

The night Adi Da was given a simple video camera, during the shooting of *Metrix* at the end of March 2001, he incorporated it on the spot. His first new video suite, *The Acrylic Block*, presented moving color footage created in conjunction with the black-and-white photographs. A few days later, Adi Da expanded his use of video while creating *The Eternal Vigil of Monumental Art*. First, he projected onto the wall a photograph of the now-vacant niches in Afghanistan where ancient Buddhist statues had recently been destroyed. Next, he projected onto the ceiling a photograph of the statues in their original form. Finally, Adi Da photographed and videoed human subjects dancing on square platforms in front of the empty niches. In the soundtrack of the accompanying video suite, *Ordinary Buddhas*, Adi Da is heard saying, "All the stone Buddhas have vacated their niches. Now, all you ordinary buddhas must fill the spaces."

From then on, video work became an integral part of Adi Da's process and aesthetic. Virtually overnight, he had mastered the new technology and started to push its limits—while always serving his primary communication of the transcending of "point of view".

For Adi Da, video footage became a new potential for recording a continuously shifting view of the subject. He also made use of an array of video effects, from negative colors to posterizing to specialized layering and feedback, elevating them to new aesthetic heights.

The exaggerated colors Adi Da used in his videography are the first examples of his intentionally non-naturalistic work with color. The unique vibratory nature of each hue, Adi Da has explained, has a different effect on the being, and his colors are chosen on that basis. Such unexpected color combinations are a further means to bring the viewer beyond what is ordinary and familiar.

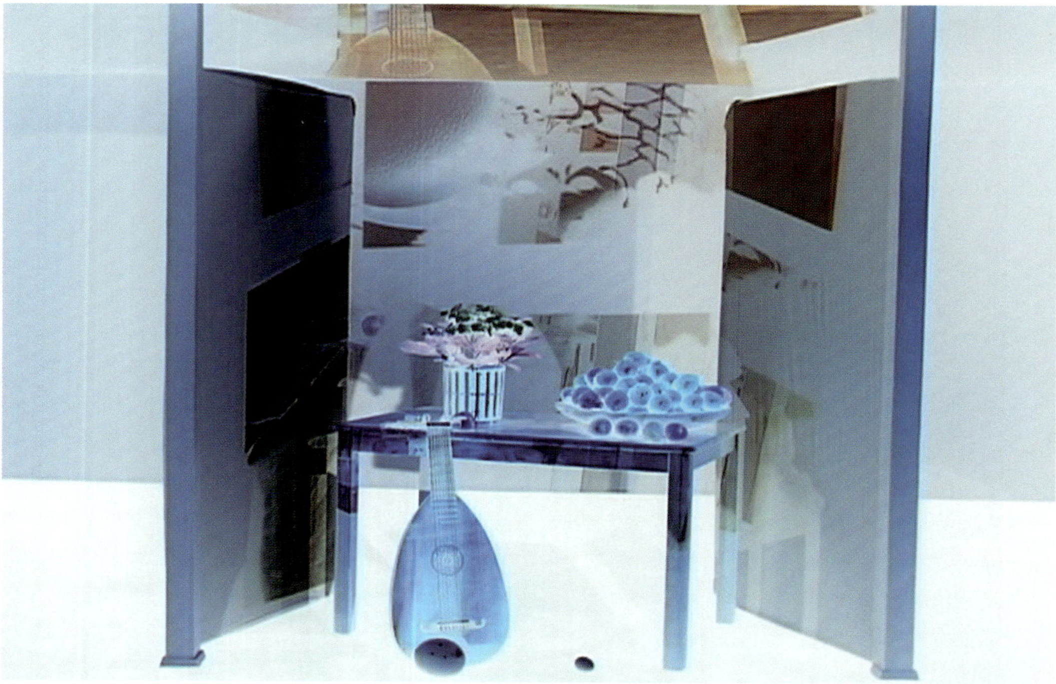

*Already Silent Without Thinking*, 2001.
Single frame.

When making his video suites *The Accident of Beauty* and *Already Silent Without Thinking*, Adi Da spoke of working with the still-life tradition of Cézanne, Picasso, and Braque. With bowls of oranges and apples, vases of flowers, a guitar, and a lute, Adi Da composed a room of archetypal objects in exquisite arrangement. Adi Da's video suites of still lifes, however, often include a nude-in-motion, an addition to the scene that seems to deny the ideal of the "perfect moment in time". The three walls enclosing the set are clearly artificial. Furthermore, Adi Da decided at this point to make video stills—chosen in intervals from throughout the many hours of tape—as yet another art form. Thus, his work with video in many ways posed the question: What is moving and what is still?

By *Fun House*—the most elaborate set of this period—Adi Da had developed video to a highly sophisticated degree. The set of *Fun House*—which also became the set of *The Balloon Theory of Everything*, the video suite associated with *Fun House*—took up every inch of the building. With multiple video cameras Adi Da created a highly complex environment of "real" walls and objects, as well as projected planes of light and dimension. The Coney Island artifacts lent an eerie color palette to his work.

Subsequent suites, on sets that were even more technically elaborate, always included video capability. A unique work created via the videographic medium was *How She Looks*, a compositional tour-de-force spontaneously made in a single afternoon, with one female subject in a kitchen, and a countertop array of fruits, vegetables, and flowers.

Ever-increasing technical complexity is a characteristic pattern in Adi Da's artistic process over the years. However, for Adi Da, the primacy of the relation to the subject, the communication beyond "point of view", and the purity of aesthetics are always senior to the technical equipment. As part of this principle of the seniority of the aesthetic dimension, Adi Da also has assistants in his art-making to fulfill certain practical and technical needs, thereby enabling him to remain concentrated in the creating of images. The assistants are not creative collaborators—he alone determines every aspect of every artwork. As in a medieval guild, Adi Da is master artist, with circles of administrative and technical assistants around him. For these assistants, serving Adi Da's artistic process is understood to be a remarkable opportunity to be grown in every dimension of the being.

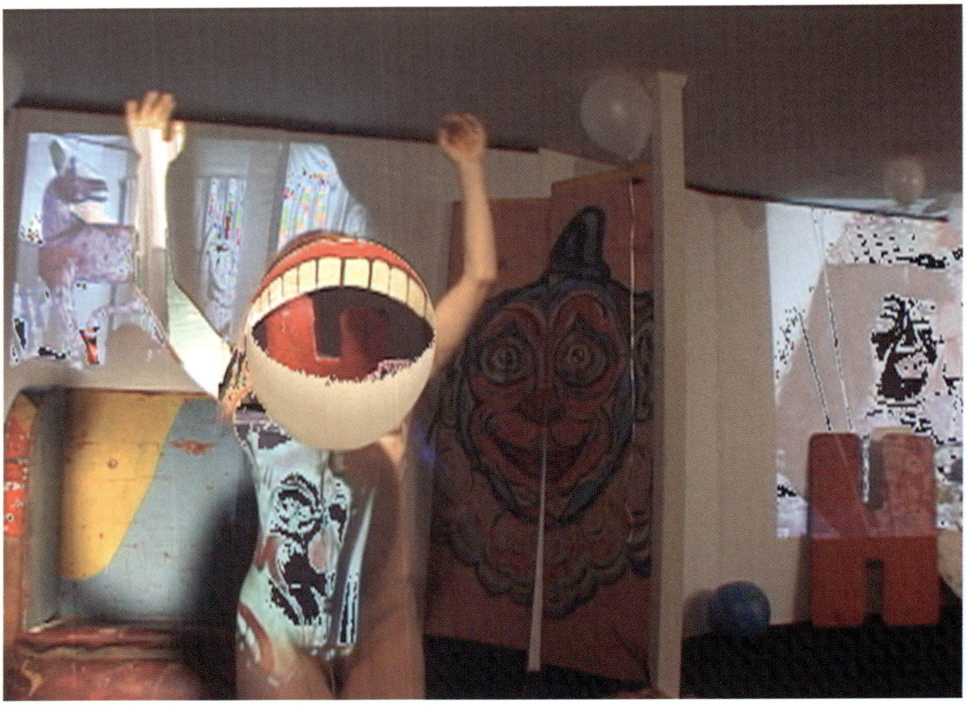

*The Balloon Theory of Everything*, 2001.
Single frame.

## ADI DA SAMRAJ: VIDEOGRAPHIC SUITES

March–September 2001

*The Acrylic Block* (associated with *Metrix: The Binary Thaw*).

*Spherical Geometry.*

*Ordinary Buddhas* (associated with *The Eternal Vigil of Monumental Art*).

*The Revelation Analog: A Binary Intensification of the Original Idea of the Rose* (associated with *The Analog of Flora Mata*).

*The Accident of Beauty.*

*Already Silent Without Thinking* (associated with *The Re-Birth of the Idea of Oranges*).

*The Balloon Theory of Everything: After the Spherical Rose Has Fallen from the Ceiling into the Body's Room of Mind* (associated with *Fun House*).

*How She Looks.* A Still Video Suite of 2,338 images.

*Happenine Flora.*

CHAPTER SEVEN

# Overwhelming Views: Monumental Fabrications

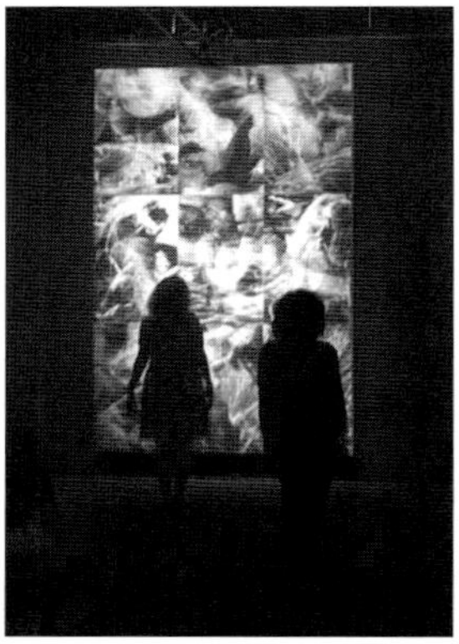

Despite the extraordinary artistic and technical efforts Adi Da Samraj puts into creating his images, he never considers them final artworks until they are produced in material—and, most often, very large-scale—two- and three-dimensional forms. Once his "source-images" are composed and preserved on film or in digital form, Adi Da considers them "coded artifacts", or "blueprints", from which fabrications are to be generated—"like a score for music, a pattern yet to be realized in tangible form".

Adi Da Samraj values monumental size for his works as a means to overwhelm the viewer and assist the process of participation beyond the ordinary use of the mind. Thus, he generally requires his fabrications to be larger than the physical body, in order to change the relationship of the viewer to the art.

*I work to transcend the egoic limitations inherent in the mechanism of "point of view". Therefore, that work is not accomplished finally until the fabrication occurs. My images are not merely intellectual images. They are not merely "mind-sized" or "head-sized". They confront the person by being bigger than the body. They require an adaptation, an adjustment, a response that even transcends the usual body-mind limitations.*

*Part of the purpose of the monumentality of size is being confronted by the art—enclosed, surrounded. My art is beyond your own scale. You cannot put it in your hand. You cannot fit it into your mind. You have to deal with it. The art is dealing with you, in some sense.*

*My image-art is always about going beyond any merely conceptual interpretation. The fabrication of an image I have made is a tangible "something", not merely a conceptual "something".*

*Fundamentally, I am working in the medium of light—but I am not working in light divorced from tangibility. My work is not merely a conceptual exercise.*

In terms of media, Adi Da draws on a diversity of materials with which to fabricate his images. Among the mandates for his fabrications are seamlessness and the lack of frames—in other words, no breaking of the image, or separating it from the space surrounding it.

The fabrications process is also an example of Adi Da's use of guilds as an extension of his unique technical methodology. In his essay, "My Material Art Must Forever Remain Within The Perfect Room", in *Transcendental Realism: The Image-Art of egoless Coincidence with Reality Itself*, Adi Da describes his need to remain focused in the purity and time-intensiveness of his source-image creation. Therefore, he indicates that all aspects of the hands-on construction, business administration, and marketing of his art are "to be done by fully skilled, responsively enthusiastic, and exactly careful professionals". By delegating such responsibilities to others, and by choosing not to appear in public to promote his art, Adi Da is able to maintain his life of spiritual retreat as a renunciate.

## The Room as Art

The exhibitions of Adi Da's fabrications are total-environment installations, in which the viewer experiences multiple monumental forms in different media simultaneously. To aid the viewer in the deepest, undistracted participation in his images, Adi Da has often created entirely windowless, black spaces in which to experience his art. The disorientation of entering such a space is the artist's intentional purpose.

*My impulse artistically is to surround people with art, to bring them into a space that is the art-work I make, not just into a room where the art is somehow under control or made into décor, or where the viewer is in control of the art.*

*The viewer should not be in control of the art. It is not that the art is "attacking" them—but it certainly is about being unable to size it down to your size, enclose it, control it, talk about it, think about it, interpret it, or abstract yourself from it. The viewer should be too busy dealing with the art I make to think about it.*

## First Galleries and Performances

In April 2001, Adi Da's first monumental fabrications—images from his suite *The Reassertion of Perfume in the Instant of Time*—were displayed in a large gallery space at the Mountain Of Attention retreat sanctuary. These five-by-seven-foot ink prints on canvas fulfilled the "paintings in light" on a "monumental" scale he had envisioned for so long.

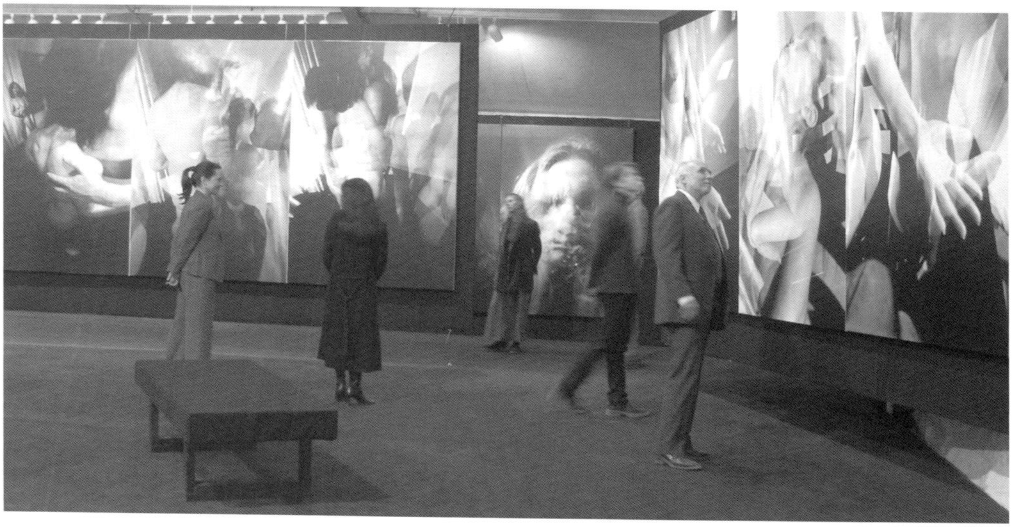

The "Bright" Room Gallery, The Mountain Of Attention Sanctuary, 2001.

Later that year, a much larger gallery space was created by erecting a tent near the entrance to the property, the interior entirely lined in black. Here, Adi Da established what he came to call "The 'Bright' Room Gallery", creating a space where more than one form of his artistic work could be experienced simultaneously. The largest wall held giant compositions up to fifteen feet high, while an opposite wall provided the large screens for a projected form of viewing his suites. In other parts of the gallery, rotating lightboxes and panels of lit imagery augmented the large-scale prints on canvas.

This period of Adi Da's work was a prolific explosion of suites and monumental fabrications—so he needed a way to immediately view and present his rapidly expanding body of images. A few years earlier, he had developed a performance-art "ceremony" for presenting his images. A timed procession of presenters dressed in black carried the large prints, bringing them up close to seated viewers. The number of images in this "moving gallery" was much greater than what could be hung in the physical space. Moreover, the event was naturally participatory. The larger-than-the-head scale and personal contact with each image met Adi Da's essential principles for receiving his art.

By 2001, Adi Da was creating at such a speed that prints were out of the question for readily presenting his work. The new form of what he called "the 'Bright' Room Ceremony" used three screens, three projectors, and loud, often percussive music to aid "unguarded" participation in his art. In this unique period of his artistic process, Adi Da originally performed every ceremony as a live event, operating a remote to move from one group of images to the next, in rhythm to the music. The sheer volume of Adi Da's creative output was so great that these became weekly events, with up to two hundred people in attendance—virtual all-night happenings. The screenings gave Adi Da and the viewers access to great quantities of his images. And the screened versions of the suites became, in and of themselves, one of the forms of monumental fabrication.

## A Monumental Vision

When an image comes to the point of fabrication, it may go through myriad changes as Adi Da responds to the particular circumstance of the event, the place, the audience, and the exhibition. Adi Da's interactive process of fabricating his images aligns to his seminal principle of participation as the basis for all true art. For Adi Da, this living, interactive exchange is primary to the meaning and purpose of the art itself.

At the time of this publication, Adi Da has created over 74,000 source-images, yet only a tiny fraction have been materially fabricated. Adi Da's written descriptions of fabrications of every kind and of total-sensory, "transformational" exhibitions fill volumes. Given the means, no space is too large for his vision.

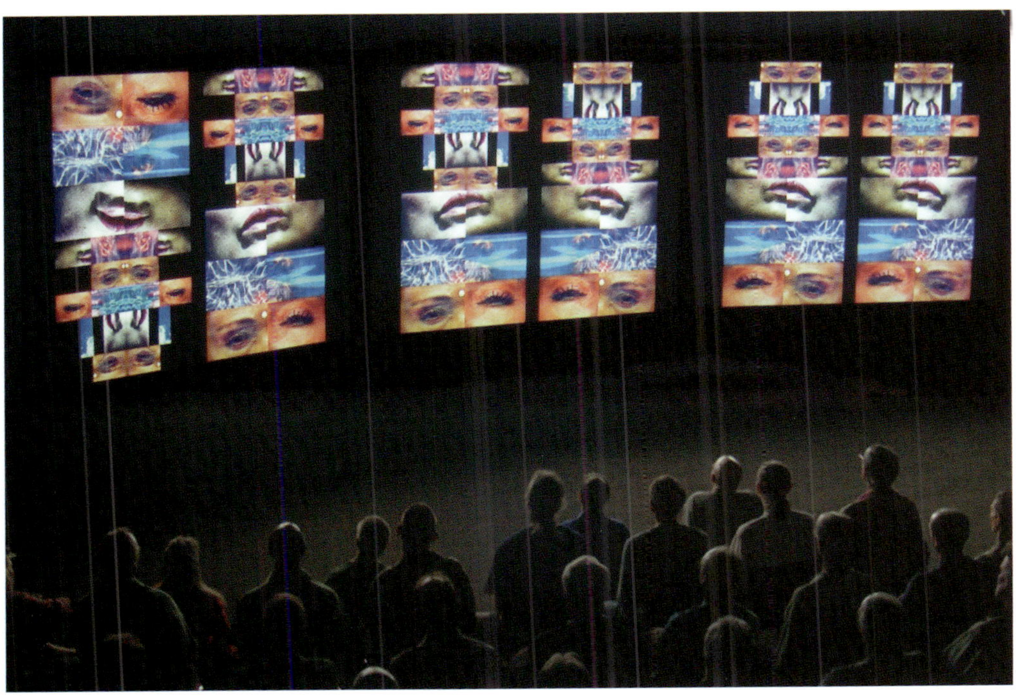

Screened showing of *The Breather*,
The "Bright" Room Gallery, The Mountain Of Attention Sanctuary, 2003.

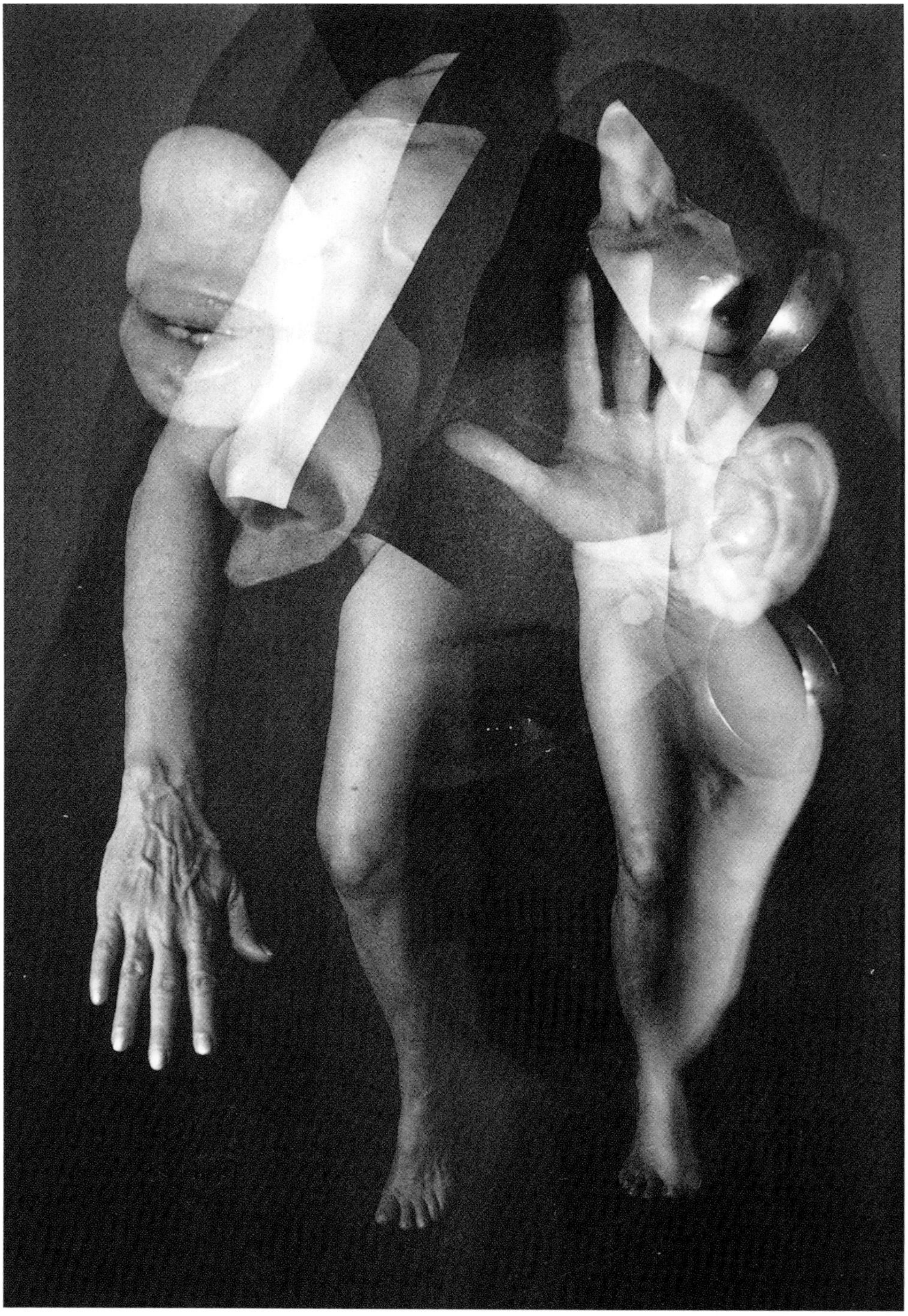

*Happenine*, 2001.
Single Image.

CHAPTER EIGHT

# Infinite Views: Images in the Thousands

In July 2001, Adi Da moved back to an indoor set, to the high-ceilinged living room of the house above Clear Lake, and began to shoot again with subjects, props, and movable walls. The intensity of his work began to build as well, with increased technical complexity, grueling hours on the set, and suites which took weeks to make, numbering in the thousands of images. The work from this period represents Adi Da's corpus of photographic epics, visual feasts of philosophical magnitude and potency.

Addressing themes such as death, the search for bodily fulfillment, and the futility of mental knowledge, these suites are bold commentaries on the human dilemma. Vast abstract narratives, each work has its own unique language and structure. But they are all intended to monumentally overwhelm the separative "point of view", in both meaning and massiveness.

## *Happenine* and *Odalisque*

Early in his work on the new indoor set, Adi Da began to experiment with further ways to isolate part of the subject in a photographic frame, a technique he had often used in the past. For several days, Adi Da called subjects up to his lens at top speed, capturing an eye, nose, mouth, ear, or leg, building collages of body parts, patterned fabrics and props—up to ten layers on the film. As the rolls were developed, striking yet unsettling visions of fierce entities, reminiscent of the Laughing Mama of *Fun House*, took form. In the final weeks of his work on this new suite, *Happenine*, Adi Da began his daily sessions by choosing props from among dozens of handmade white masks he had laid out in rows on the floor. *Fun House*–like elements, such as balloons, carnival figures, and a free-standing clown, also returned to his visual language.

Adi Da's next opus, *Odalisque: The Myth of the Reclining Woman*, is his play on the art-historical archetype of the reclining nude, found in both East and West since antiquity. His purpose was to counter the "myth of satisfaction" that the odalisque represents.

*The odalisque figure traditionally represents the passively attractive woman—the woman who is to be looked at, who is beautiful, desirable, who is sexually available even, in one mode or another.*

*I intend this suite to serve a fundamental profundity of awareness relative to life and death, relative to desire and the search for pleasure—and, of course, the ultimate unsatisfactoriness of the search for pleasure, the ultimate impossibility of egoic fulfillment.*

*My communication in this suite, however, is not merely about despair. It is a very complex matter, done through visual images rather than through verbal explanation.*

## *9 Mary* and *She Is Mind*

*9 Mary: The Superconductivity of Celibate Women Under the Midnight Sun*, the next of Adi Da's works, was a pinnacle in his black-and-white imagery, employing innovative uses of video and projection as means to veil, unveil, and "re-pattern" nine female subjects in light. A compositional form of nine images, which he named the "nonaptych" (in horizontal or other arrangements), became the structural aesthetic for the suite. When the shooting was done, the sequencing of the tremendous number of images—over 2,300—required great stamina and a great amount of space. Networks of rooms filled with mazes of easels were assembled for Adi Da to hand-arrange the 5″ x 7″ prints, standing on his feet for hours every day over a period of several weeks. In his sequencing, Adi Da always worked with a suite as a whole, while also meticulously making the complex aesthetic decisions to weave each image into the fabric of the entirety.

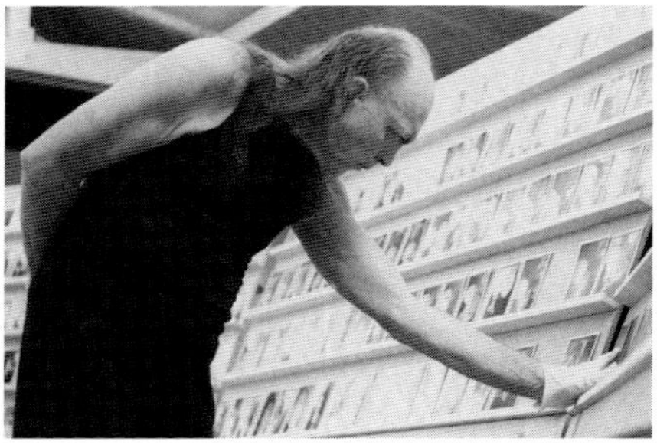
Adi Da Samraj sequencing images, 2001.

Once again, Adi Da's artistic process had a direct correlation to the meaning of his work: In *9 Mary*, his primary communication was "diversity within unity". At the conclusion of every body of his screened image-art, Adi Da's representation of the "midnight sun" appears, visually resolving all apparent separateness in the ultimate unity of all.

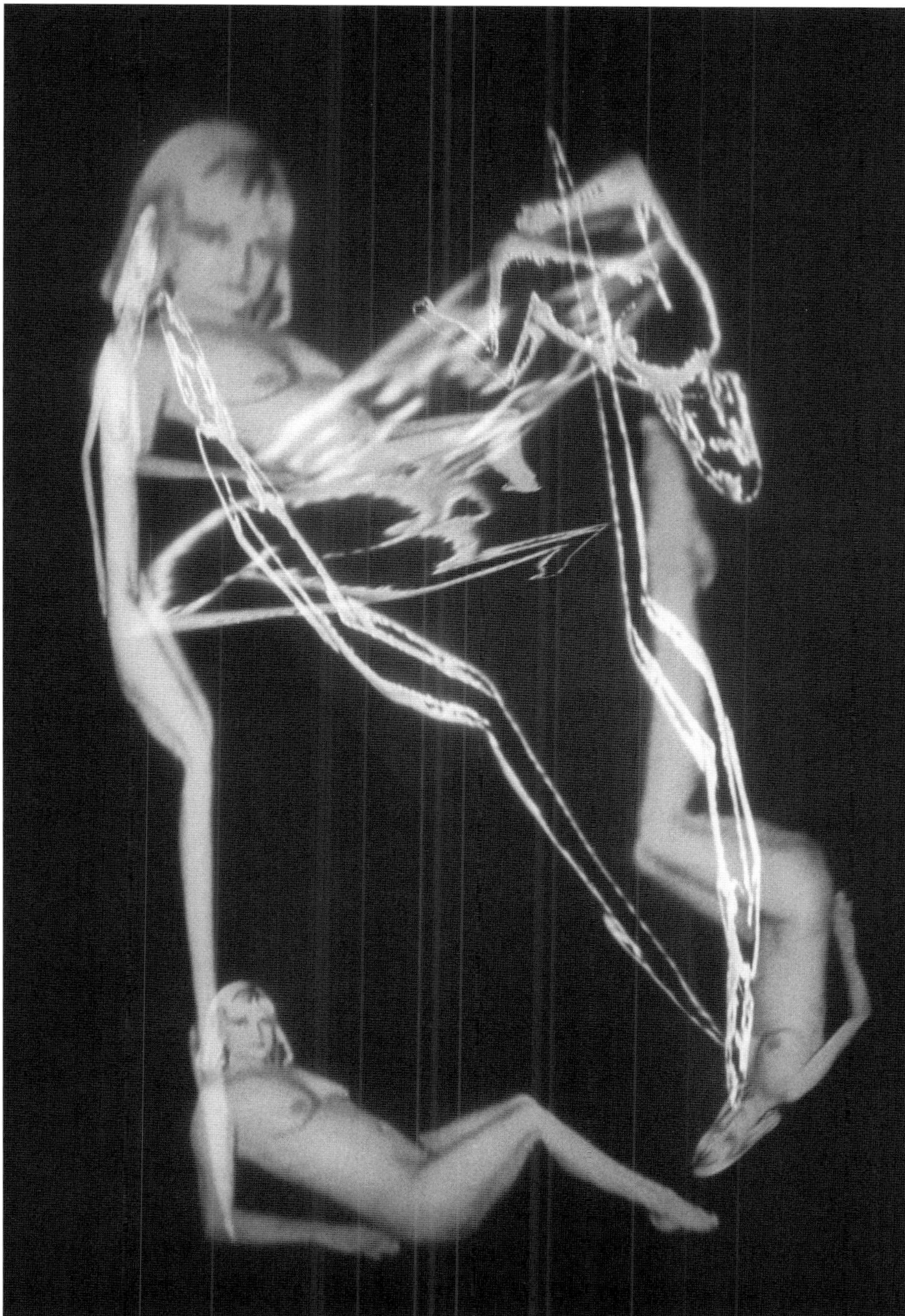

*Odalisque*, 2001.
Single Image.

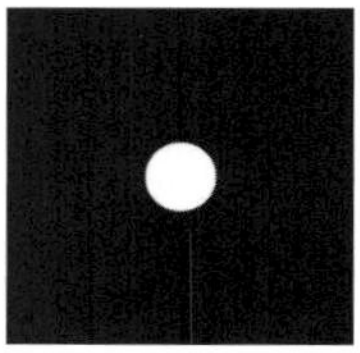

Adi Da's visual representation of the "Midnight Sun".

*The entire cosmic domain is a field—indeed, it may appropriately be imagined as a cube—of black, with all perceptions and conceptions gone. In the midst of that black cube, there is a Sphere that looks like the Full Moon—but with no features or patterns on the face of It. Its Radiance is like that of the Sun, rather than the Moon. Yet, there is Great Pleasure in beholding It—unlike the physical Sun, which is impossible to look at, with its rays and brilliance. This Eternal "Midnight Sun" Is the Direct and Tangible Entrance from the night sky of the body-mind Into What Is Beyond the black.*

*The "Midnight Sun" Is the Hole in the universe. It is Divine Being objectified. When there is passage into That Place (or the Divine Self-Condition Itself), there is nothing more to say.**

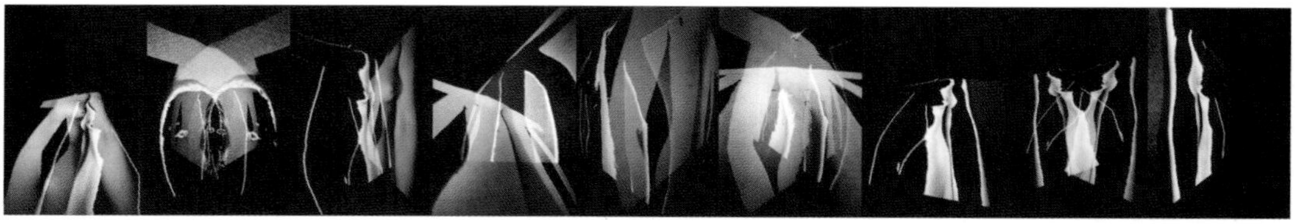

9 *Mary*, 2001–2002.
Horizontal Nonaptych.

*From *Eleutherios (The Only Truth That Sets The Heart Free)*, by Adi Da Samraj (Middletown, CA: The Dawn Horse Press, 2006).

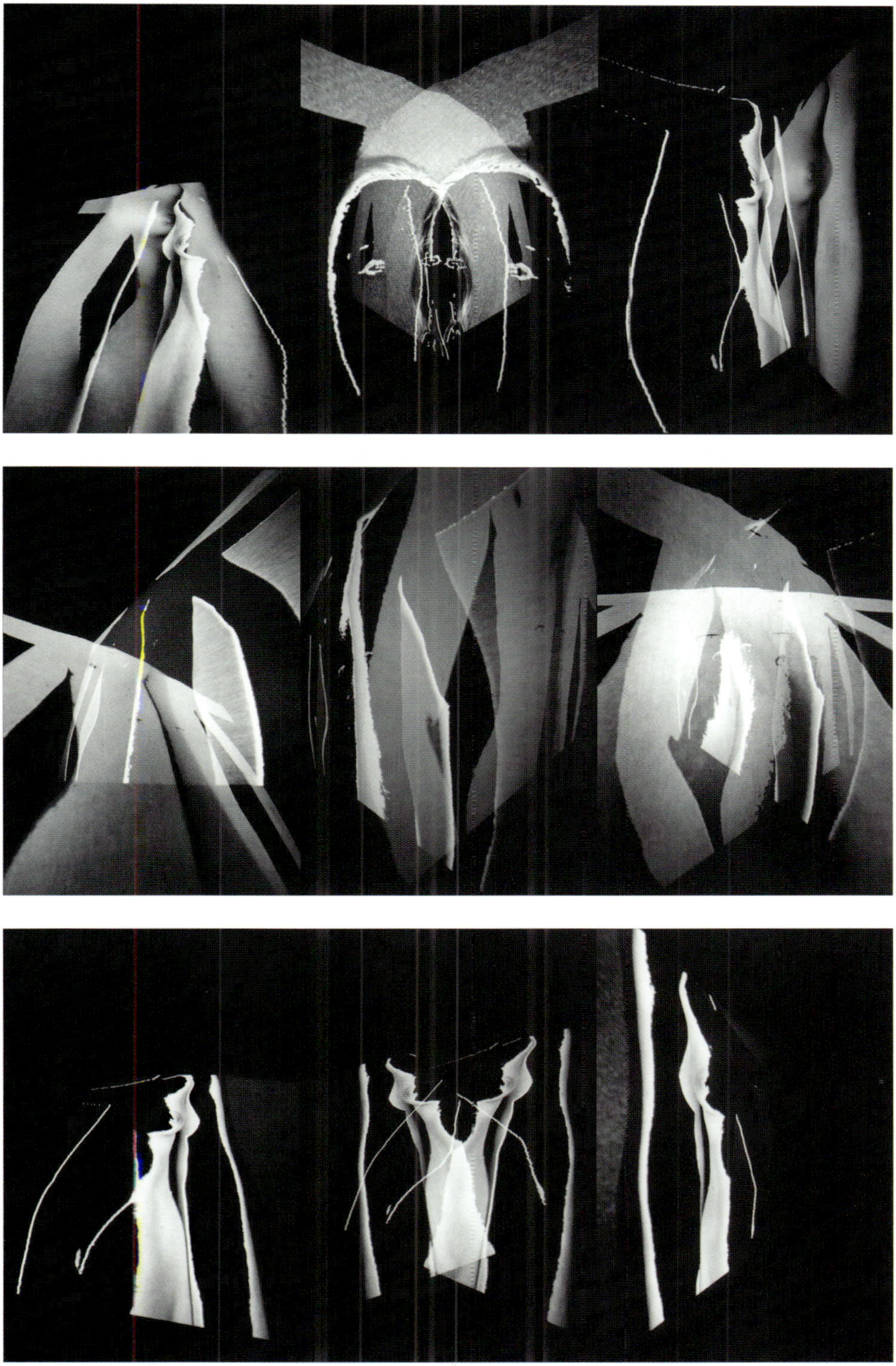

*9 Mary,* 2001–2002.
Horizontal Nonaptych from facing page, shown here as three triptychs.

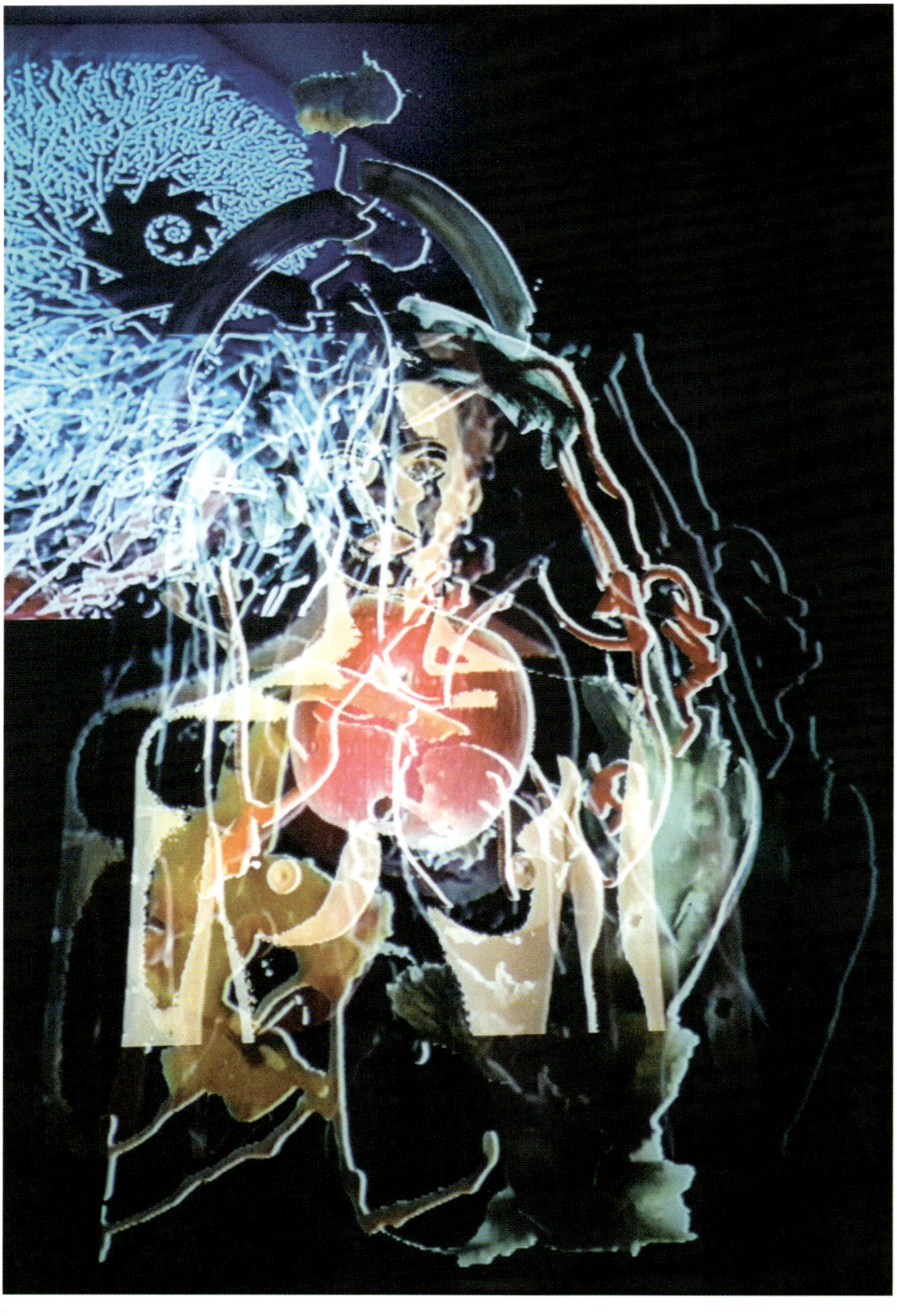

*She Is Mind*, 2002.
Single color Image.

*9 Mary* was completed in January 2002. Adi Da lost no time, starting in less than a month on his next suite. *She Is Mind: The Iconography of Eve* was yet another leap in complexity of meaning and technical sophistication. A new set at the Mountain Of Attention expanded Adi Da's capacity for projections and gave him access, via a database, to all of his artworks in all media. This was also the moment Adi Da chose to move into color photography. He composed this next work alternating between black-and-white and color nonaptychs—representing, respectively, how the "root-mind" and the "perceptual mind" see.

*She Is Mind* takes the apparently simple elements of "apple", "woman", "chair", "man", etc., and masterfully choreographs them into a multilayered communication about suffering, the biblical myth of *Genesis*, and the illusion of "knowing"—in sum, "the symbols, structures, and meaning of mind". Adi Da's meanings are layered throughout the images. As in *Fun House*, universal archetypes are referenced, by using objects and images from his own past. A single archetypal female model, illustrations from *The Macmillan Visual Dictionary*,* an antique Civil War chair he had refinished and owned since 1966, and his Transcendental Drawings all make appearances in the visual language.

In deciphering *She Is Mind* for others. Adi Da spoke about many of the primary symbols—adding, in summary, that "at the end, all you have is the light". He reiterated that the goal is not to come up with a verbal explanation for his art. As he pointed out, "The obsessive effort to conceptualize or explain or grasp reality is the problem with mind."

## ADI DA SAMRAJ: "EPIC" SUITES
July 2001–March 2002

*Happenine.* 1,497 Images. Black-and-white.

*Oodalisque: The Myth of the Reclining Woman—*
*A Suite of 1,845 Images Regarding the Heart's Illusion of Captivity in the Waiting Room of Body and Mind.* Black-and-white.

*9 Mary: The Superconductivity of Celibate Women Under the Midnight Sun.* 2,313 Images. Black-and-white.

*She Is Mind: The Iconography of Eve.* 2,223 Images. Black-and-white and color.

*Used by permission. © QA Digital 2002. All rights reserved. www.qadigital.com.

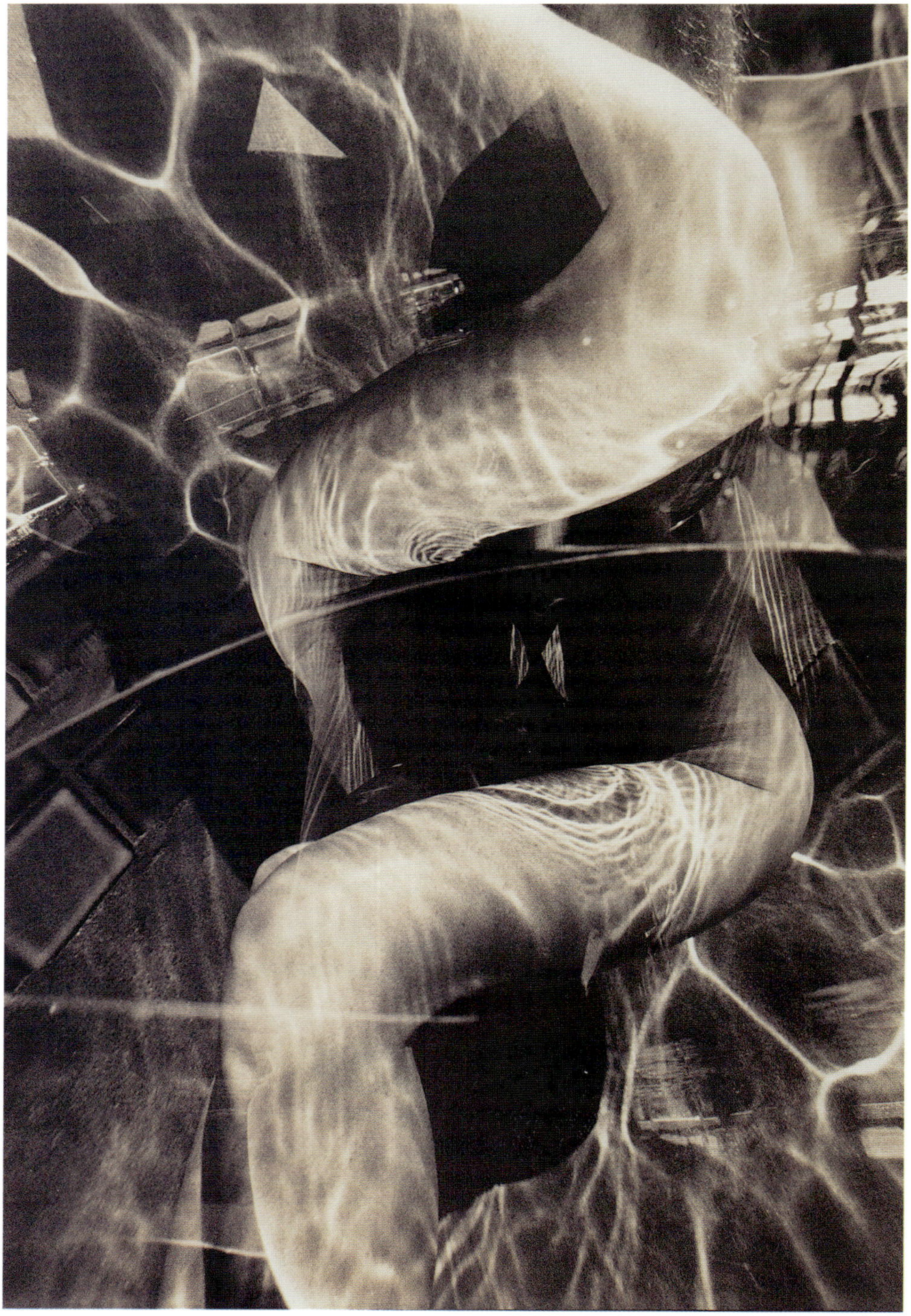

*Quandra Loka*, 2003.
Single sepia-toned Image.

# CHAPTER NINE

# Indivisible Views: Underwater Imagery

## *Quandra Loka*

In late July 2002, Adi Da Samraj moved to a small retreat circumstance on the island of Kauai in Hawaii. One day, he visited a local resort, enjoying a large, creatively landscaped swimming area. Spontaneously making use of a small disposable camera, Adi Da suddenly started making underwater photographs, creating a body of work he later called *Plastic Camera.* Once again, an entirely new phase of Adi Da's work began—this time requiring an unprecedented level of physical endurance and battle with natural elements.

For his next suite, Adi Da limited his compositions to a prescribed visual palette. He chose to work only with what could be seen in the natural setting of a garden swimming pool behind a house, in combination with one female subject. The pool had a pleasing shape, with natural rocks and a small waterfall, and the lawn was a large green expanse with palms in the distance. Soon Adi Da was living a daily discipline of five hours or more of shooting, but this time under the most extreme conditions. Underwater, he held his breath repeatedly in order to capture images of the nude form combined with light and water. He chose to free-dive, rather than wear a tank, in order to allow the greatest freedom of mobility and response to the subject. But to descend to the bottom of the pool repeatedly, Adi Da wore a cumbersome twenty-five-pound weight belt. An even greater challenge occurred when, in the midst of layering multiple exposures, Adi Da chose to leave the water, remove the belt and mask, yet remain in the stifling black neoprene suit in the intense sun and heat, in order to cross the property and capture an exposure of a leaf or sky, before returning and re-donning all the gear to make another underwater exposure—all the while holding the precise location of each of the layered exposures in his internal mental vision.

This incredible process was often interrupted by the unpredictability of the environment, such as clouds obscuring the sunlight in the middle of a frame, or debris blowing into the pool. In a victory over the forces of nature, *Quandra Loka* depicts the pristine "abode of the beloved", a rapturous symphony of color, light, and form.

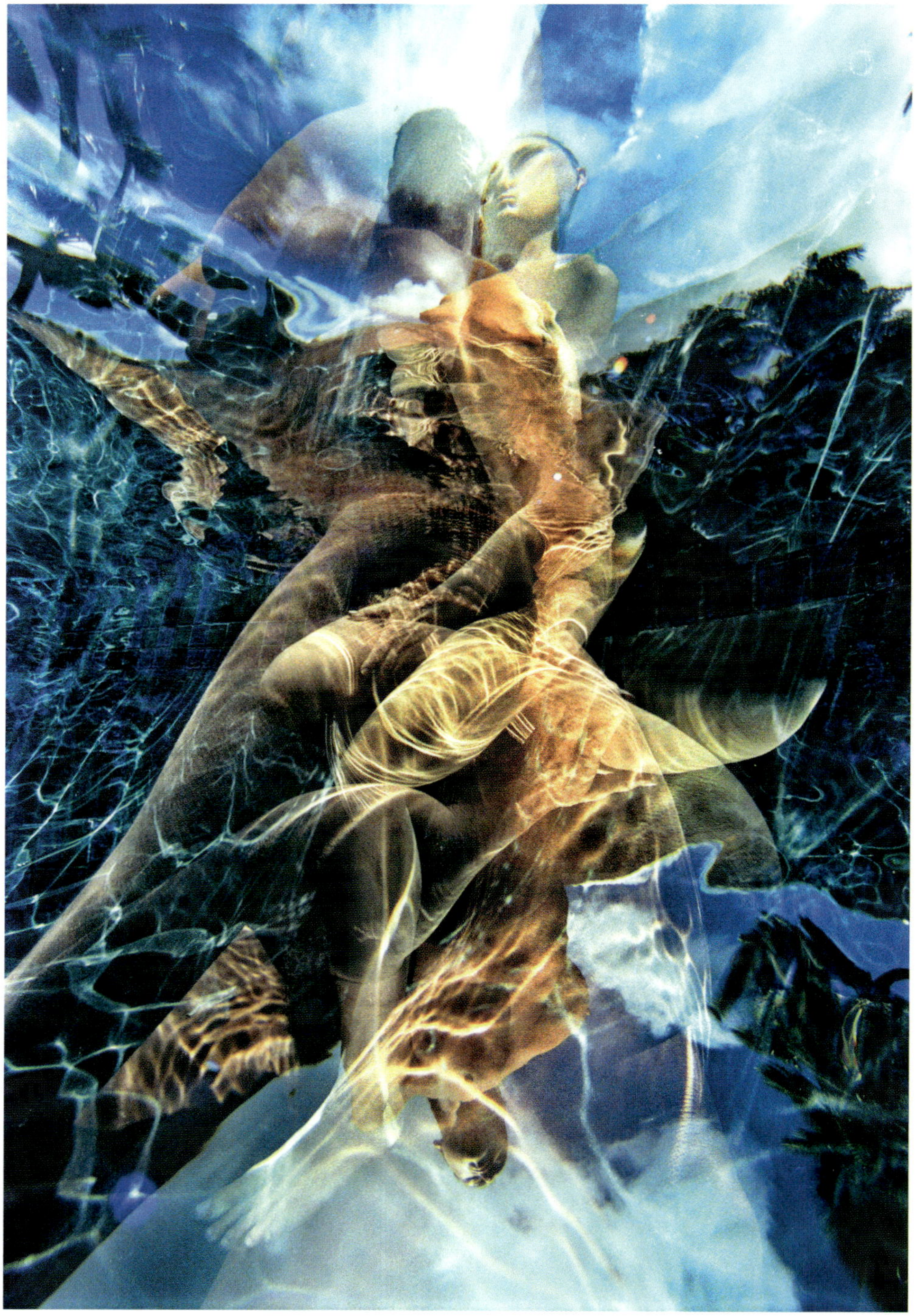

*Quandra Loka*, 2003.
Single color Image.

Quandra Loka is a visual meditation on a very simple circumstance: a woman in and near a pool of water. Narcissus, the archetype of ego, gazes at his own reflection in a pond, never able to contact the "object" of his self-enamored affection. But Quandra, the true beloved, is one with the water itself, whether in or out of the pool.

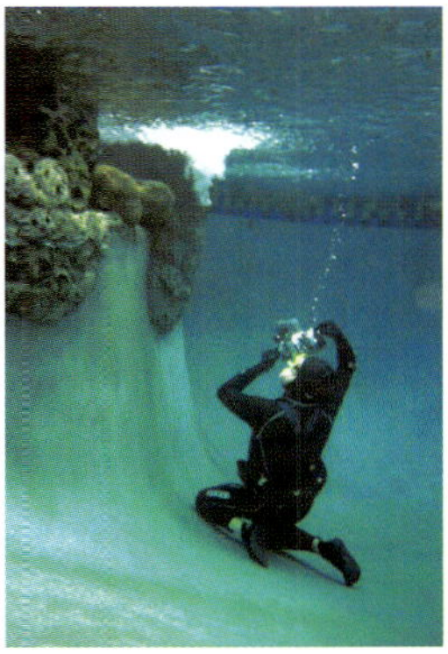

I shot the majority of the images in Quandra Loka underwater, or with the camera lens partially submerged in water, such that the water functions as a vast and subtly complex lens, achieving visual results not possible by any technical means. The images are made by a "technique" that requires continuous participation in the living instant of the photographic situation—sensitive to the constantly changing sunlight conditions, the ever-shifting minute movements of the subject, and even the ability to stay submerged underwater. This "method" is beyond conceptual effort, beyond conventions of control in the ordinary sense, beyond "point of view". This process of generating images—involving absolute awareness of every detail of what is occurring and, simultaneously, an intuitive trust in allowing the ultimately unpredictable process to take place—is a means of allowing reality to be self-manifested.

I intend these images to "picture" the unity of the undifferentiated reality from which all appearances emerge in a constant flow of changes. The entire span of human possibilities is reflected in these images—both "positive" and "negative". But all possibilities are seen in the context of that inherent unity (or indivisible space). The positives and the negatives are all transcended, rather than any attempt being made to render them acceptable in and of themselves.

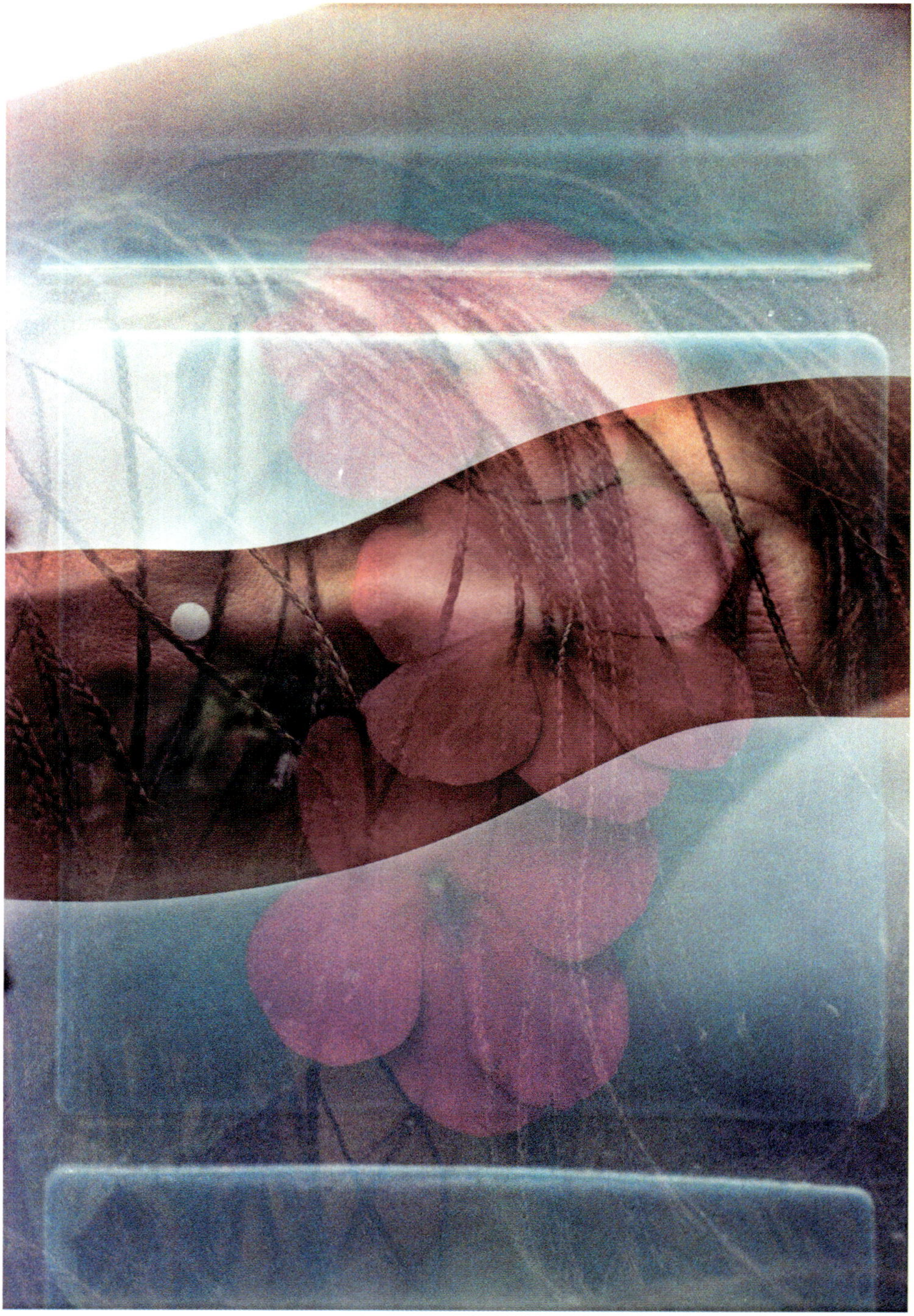

*Quandra Loka*, 2003.
Single color Image.

*Quandra Loka* became an immense suite, as Adi Da demonstrated the "infinite" combinations of his chosen simple palette. Eventually *Quandra Loka* numbered over 4,000 black-and-white images and over 1,000 in color. A collection of the black-and-white images, *The* Quandra Loka *Suite: 52 Views*, premiered at the Louis Stern Gallery in Los Angeles in April 2003, as large-scale sepia-toned inks on canvas. In the exhibition catalog essay, art critic Donald Kuspit wrote:

*Again and again, Adi Da's photographs convey a sense of aesthetic as well as physical ecstasy. Virtually all his images are masterpieces of abstraction—ecstatic visions of the female body that are simultaneously formal epiphanies.*

ADI DA SAMRAJ: "UNDERWATER" SUITES
September 2002–May 2003

*Plastic Camera I.* 268 Images. Color.

*Plastic Camera II.* 770 Images. Color.

*Quandra Loka Mille Camera I–IV.* 4,026 Images. Black-and-white.

*Quandra Loka Mille Camera V.* 1,106 Images. Color.

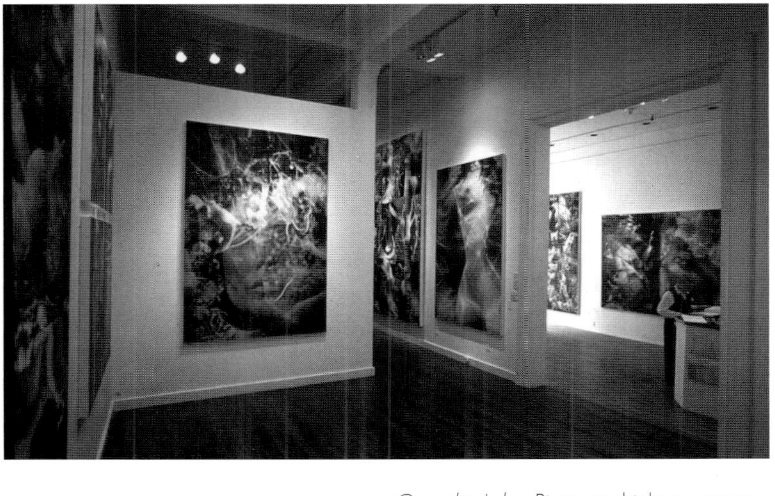

*Quandra Loka* Pigmented inks on canvas.
Louis Stern Gallery exhibition, Los Angeles, 2003.

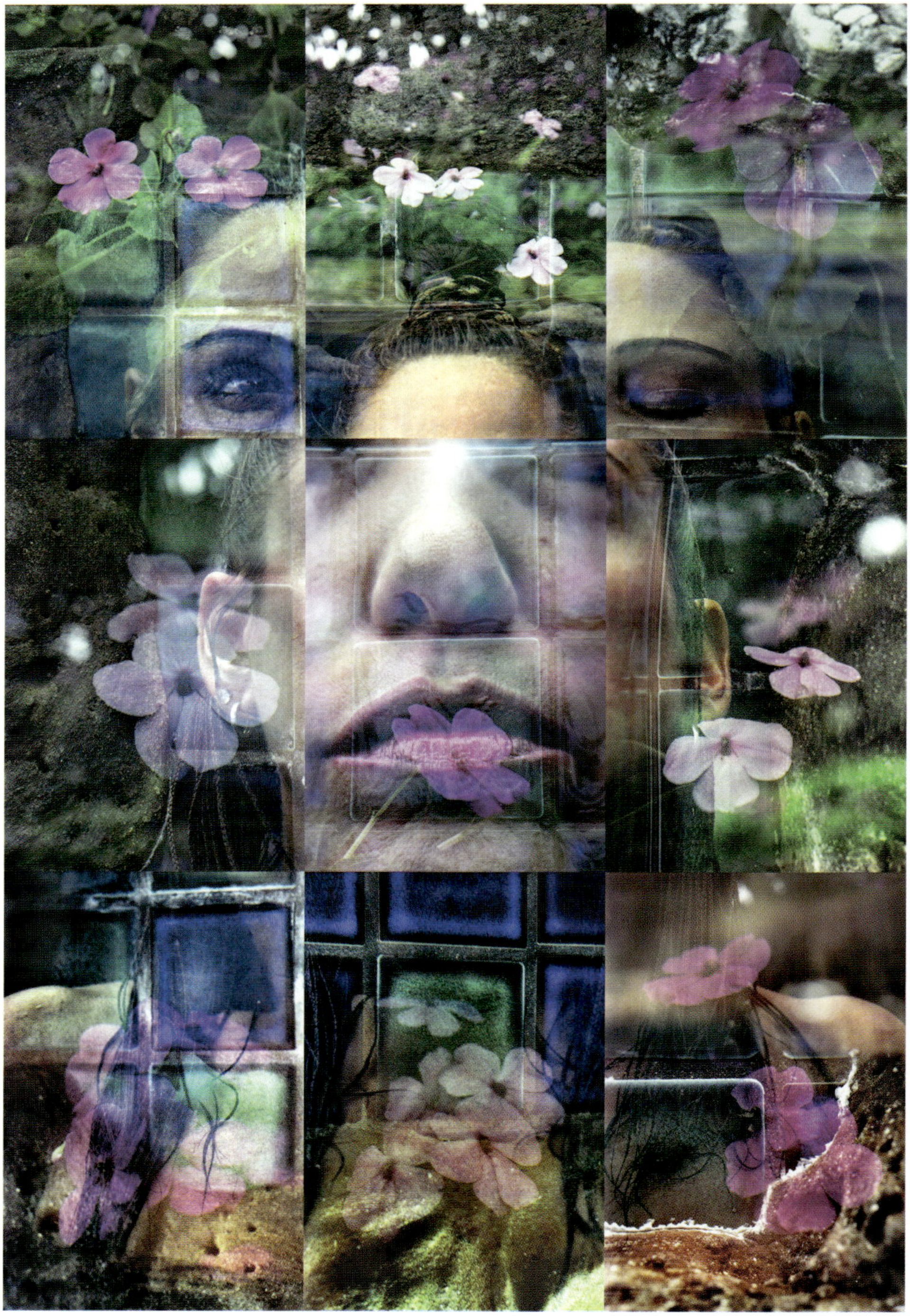

*The Breather #12*, 2003.
Nonaptych.

## CHAPTER TEN

# Juxtaposed Views: Complex Configurations

## *The Breather*

Adi Da's next exponential leap after *Quandra Loka* was to draw on this immense body of imagery and make a new form of composition. He called his mosaic-like combinations of images, in unlimited sizes and shapes, "complex configurations".

In May 2003, Adi Da Samraj returned to his island-retreat in Fiji. Even during the international travel, Adi Da worked making configurations. For the next number of months, without shooting new film, but still using *Quandra Loka* as a source, Adi Da composed his most highly complex suites to date, with images morphing from simpler arrangements into tapestries of hundreds, or even thousands, of "cells". *The Breather* was the first of these suites.

As he developed this form of artwork, Adi Da spoke of his configurations as "root-mosaics" that correspond to structures in the brain. Adi Da's comments on the brain are made on the basis of his own direct experience—and provide a possible basis for scientific investigation of perceptual processes in the brain. He invites viewers, including scientists, to contemplate his images and notice how their brains are working.

*The kind of structuring that I am doing in* The Breather *could be compared to a mosaic. It suggests something about how memory works. It tacitly puts the perceiver in touch with how experience is organized by the mind, by the brain, by the body. This kind of structuring locates something deep in the body and beyond the body.*

*The method I use to make configurations is in the mode of how the brain-mind-body works at its root-levels of perception and experiencing, prior to the fixed "separate-body" idea of the ego. My method of making configurations immediately breaks out of that ego-mold.*

The Breather *communicates at that root-level. It is purposed to draw the perceiver into a root-level of experience, and it is at that level that the meanings exist.*

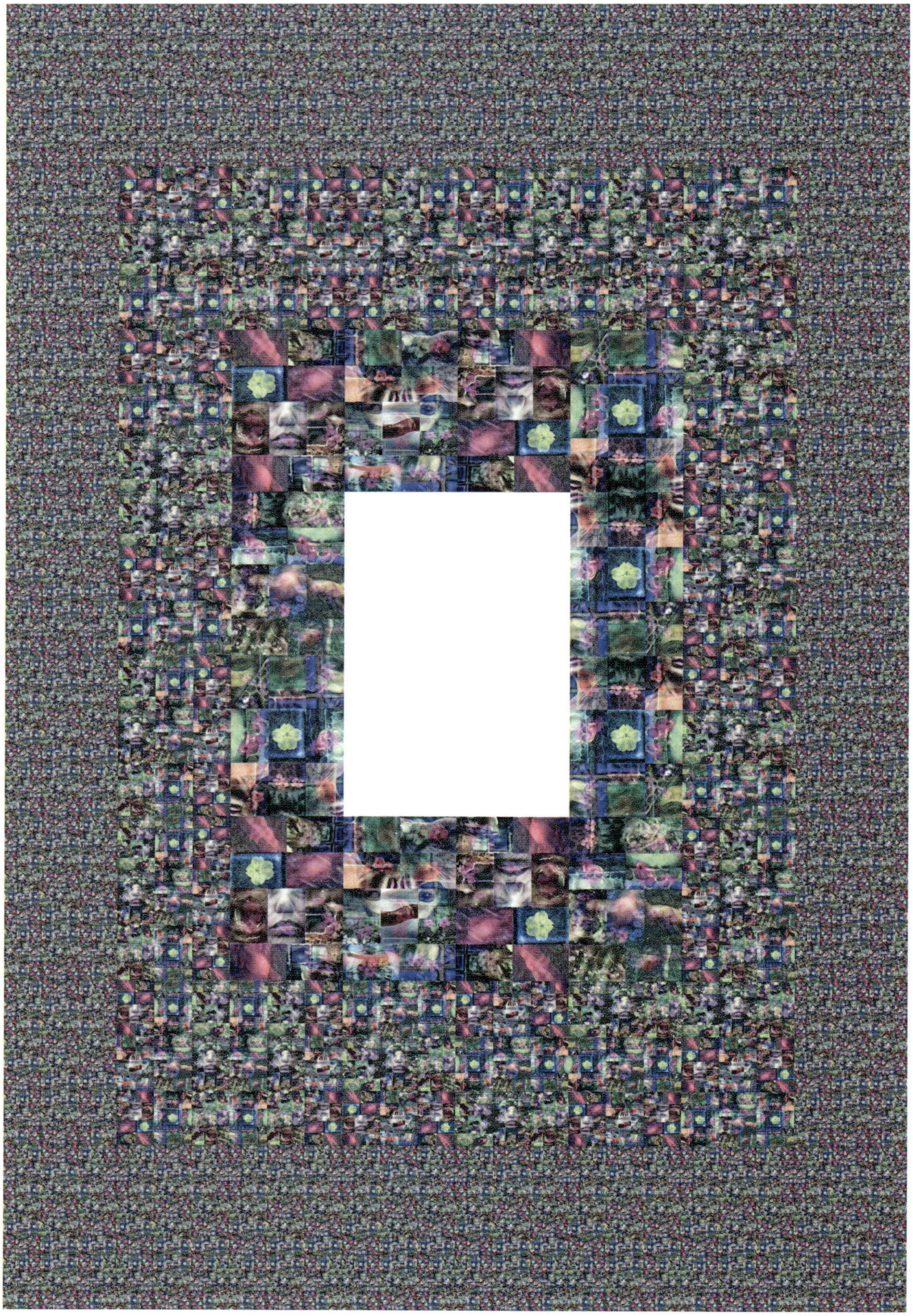

*The Breather #4346*, 2003.
Complex Configuration of over 20,000 "cells", in three different scales.

In September 2003, a configuration from *The Breather* became Adi Da's largest material fabrication to date. *The Breather #4185* premiered at the "Bright" Room Gallery in California as a fabrication over twenty feet wide. In this monumental work, Adi Da conveys the physical breath, but also "the breath as a constant process of interactive participation in the living cosmos". Ultimately, he is communicating the potential for non-separateness between the one who breathes and that which is breathed.

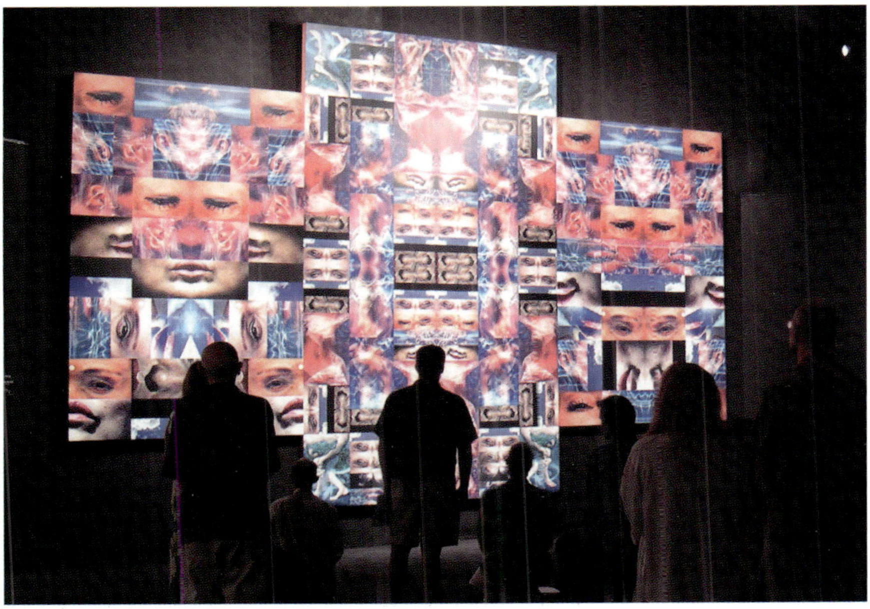

*The Breather #4185*, 2003.
Pigmented inks on canvas.
The "Bright" Room Gallery, The Mountain Of Attention Sanctuary.

## *Kaleidoscope*

For *Kaleidoscape: Eleven Visions of Countless Points of View*, Adi Da worked non-stop for weeks, completing a gargantuan suite of 6,211 complex configurations in time to premiere it on his sixty-fourth birthday that November. "Kal-eid" in Greek means "beautiful image", while "scope" means "an instrument for viewing". By changing it to "scape", Adi Da signifies the real view of the world, rather than a mirror of "pretty colored shapes" seen through the machine of "point of view".

During his work on the *Quandra Loka*–based suites, Adi Da worked with a finite number of original images to build thousands of configurations. In parts of *The Breather*, for example, a group of twenty-one frames becomes the basis for an unfolding array of seemingly endless combinative beauty. While composing *Kaleidoscape*, Adi Da made the configurations by hand, working with piles of tiny prints, which he called "chips". The guild of technicians barely kept up with Adi Da's output, rushing to record each composition and produce enough chips so he could work continuously. When Adi Da suddenly completed this phase, and moved into sequencing the more than 6,000 configurations, no one had kept track of how many base images, or single frames, he had used. He asked the guild to count. In doing so, they were astounded to discover Adi Da had composed the entire suite with only eleven frames. In response to this spontaneous outcome, Adi Da gave his suite the subtitle "Eleven Visions of Countless Points of View".

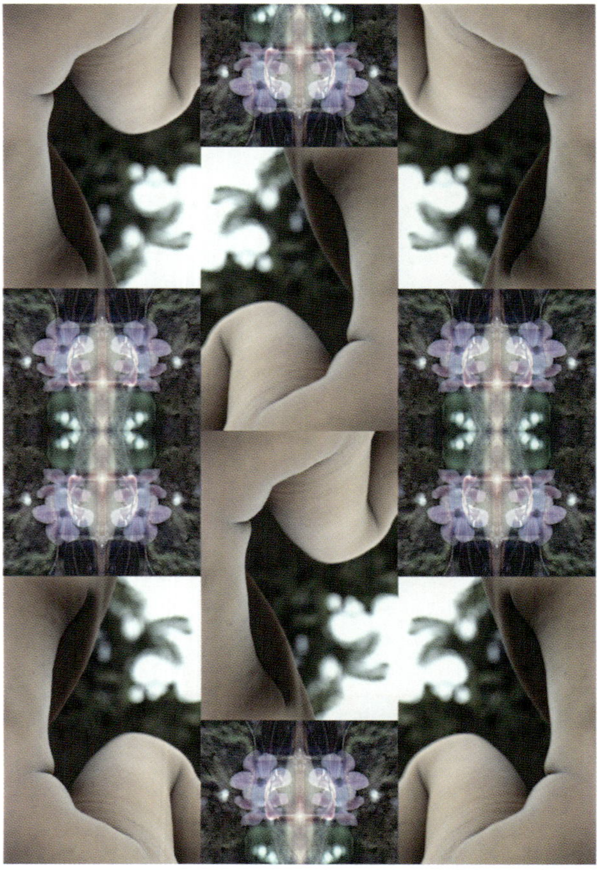

*Kaleidoscape*, 2003.
Configuration of "cells" in two different scales.

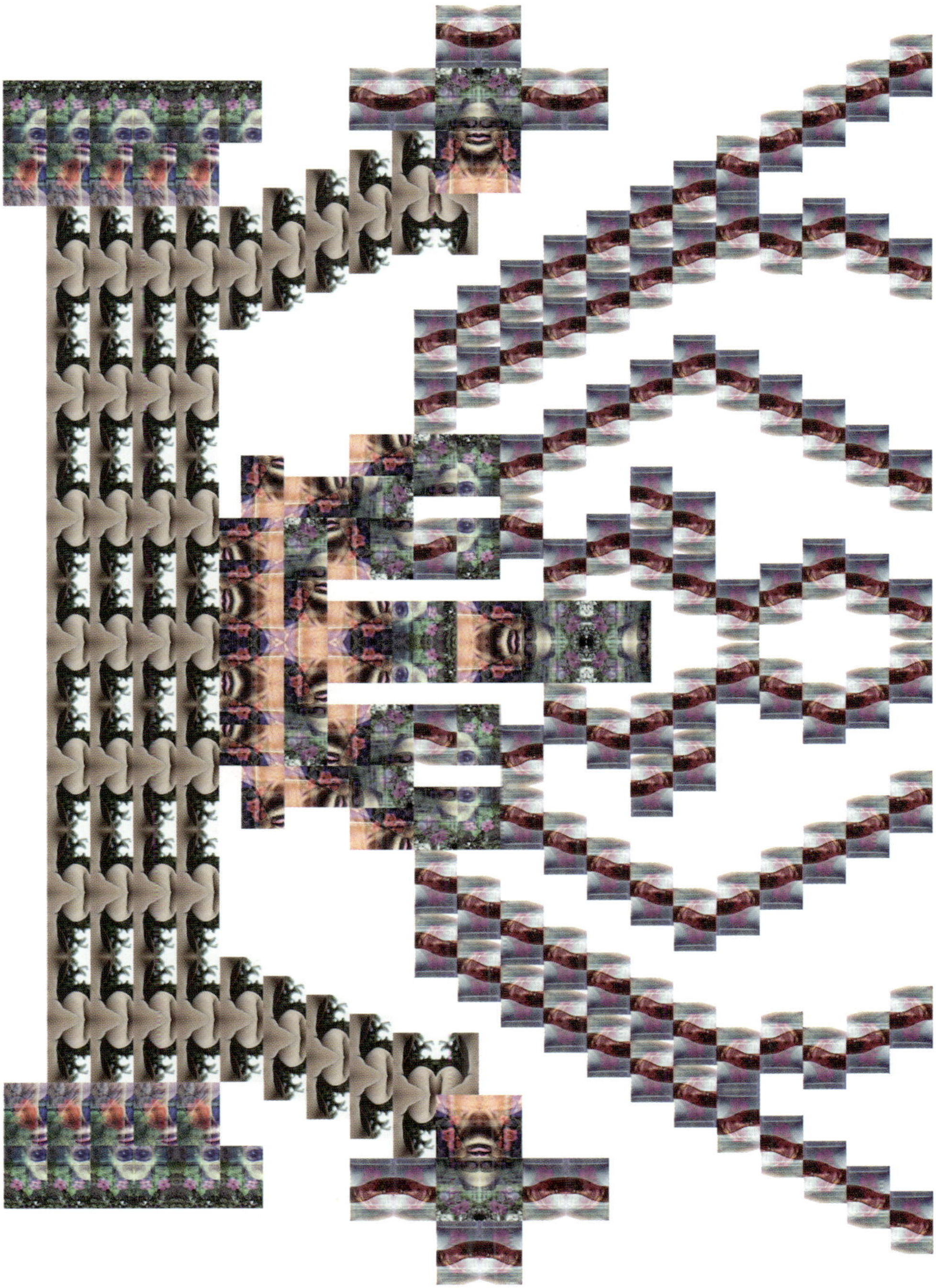

*Kaleidoscape*, 2003.
Irregularly shaped Configuration.

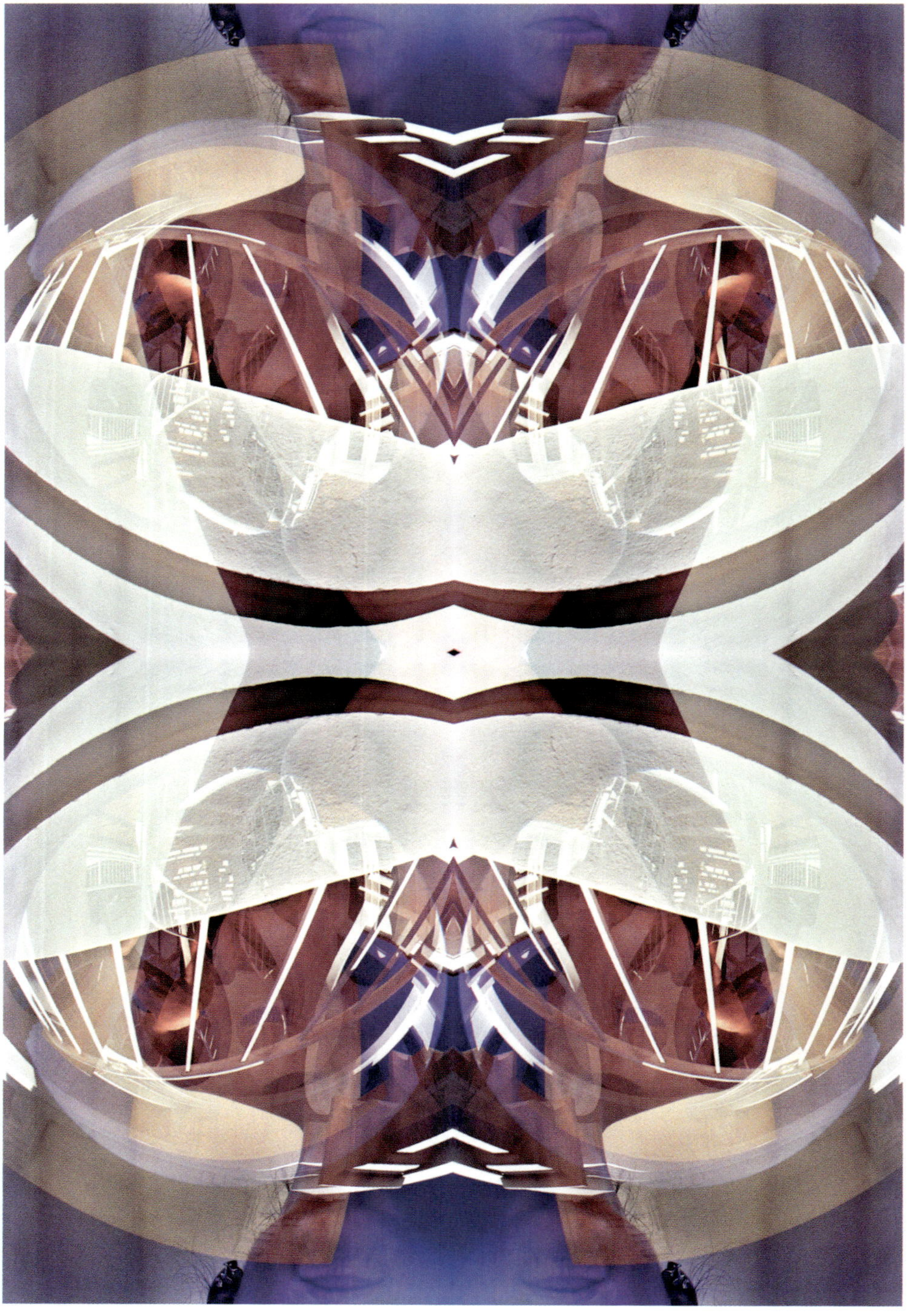

*The Spherical Tower,* 2003.
"Quadriptych" (a single frame "reflected" four times).

## Brilliance, Color, and Light

When Adi Da Samraj picked up his camera again, in October 2003, his unique new setting was a white building he had designed—with spiral staircases and tiled, arched pavilions, open to the beach and ocean. Once again, Adi Da developed a unique visual language in response to his subject and environs, and, simultaneously, a new dimension of technical innovation.

Like *Quandra Loka*, Adi Da chose for this new work, *The Spherical Tower*, a palette of elements: this time including classical vases, pedestals, tables, chairs, fruits, eggs, marble, architectural features, the ocean, sand, clouds, and the sun itself. The images were his new explorations in color, surface, and form—again using classical or modernist archetypes, but turning them into his unique commentary on the nature of reality, the fragility of the body, and the question of consciousness.

For his next work, Adi Da created an entire suite out of systematic combinations of subjects with textured surfaces. The suite, named *Three*, is a trio of female subjects fused with backgrounds of paints, tiles, and tinted grout. The effect is a startling view-shift with each surface change. The grout evokes the quality of softly painted frescoes, while the streaks of paint create a bold modernist palette. As in his earlier work, Adi Da's presentation of a face or the contoured side of a body is often unexpected and confronts the mind's effort to label or identify "who" an image is.

Employing digital tools for the first time in his artistic process, Adi Da now made use of the capability to intensify, but not replace, the original colors of the images. He saturated the photographs until they became deeply strange and non-naturalistic hues. Increasing the level of saturation revealed an incredible display of color values within the multiply-exposed layers on film.

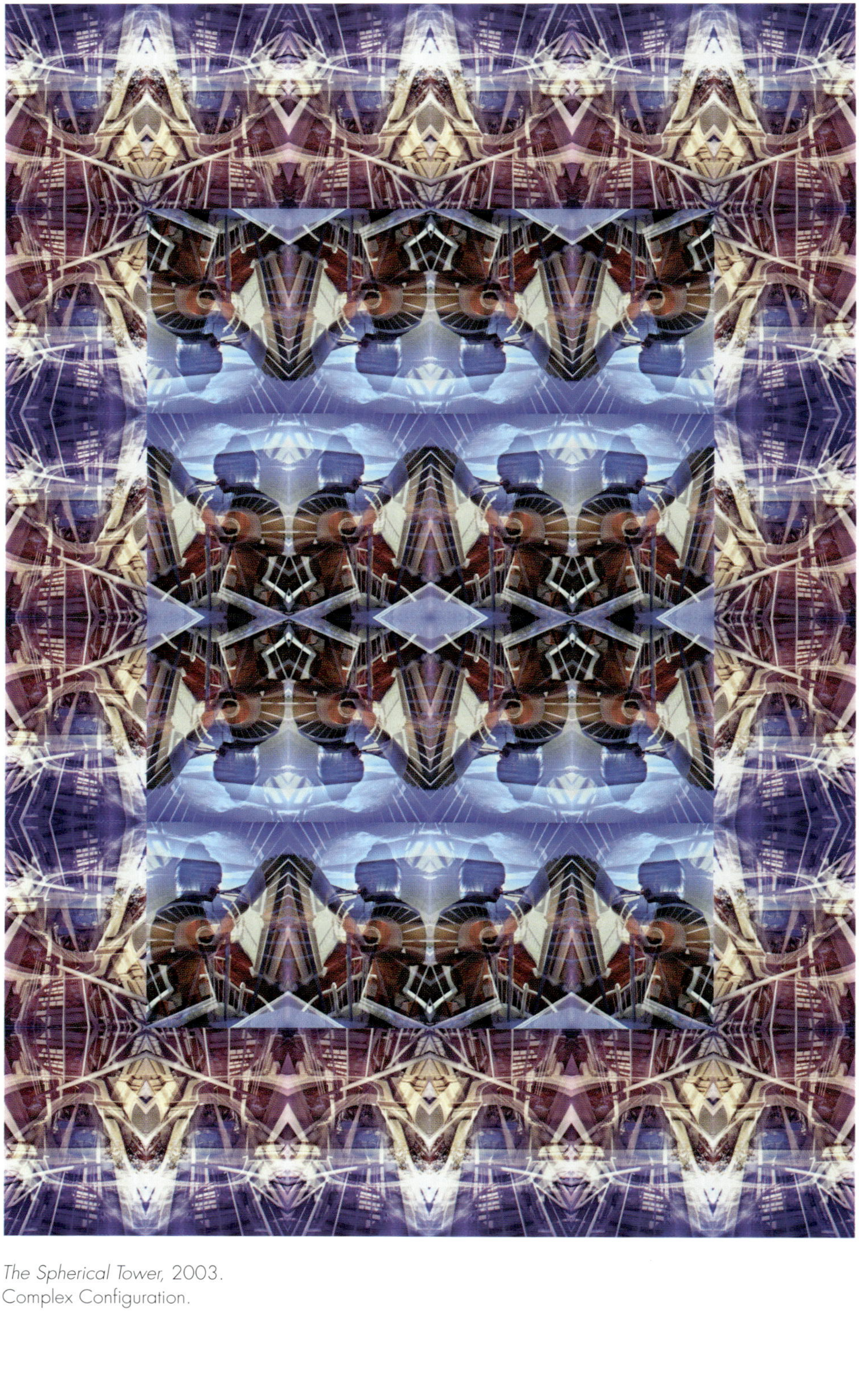

*The Spherical Tower*, 2003.
Complex Configuration.

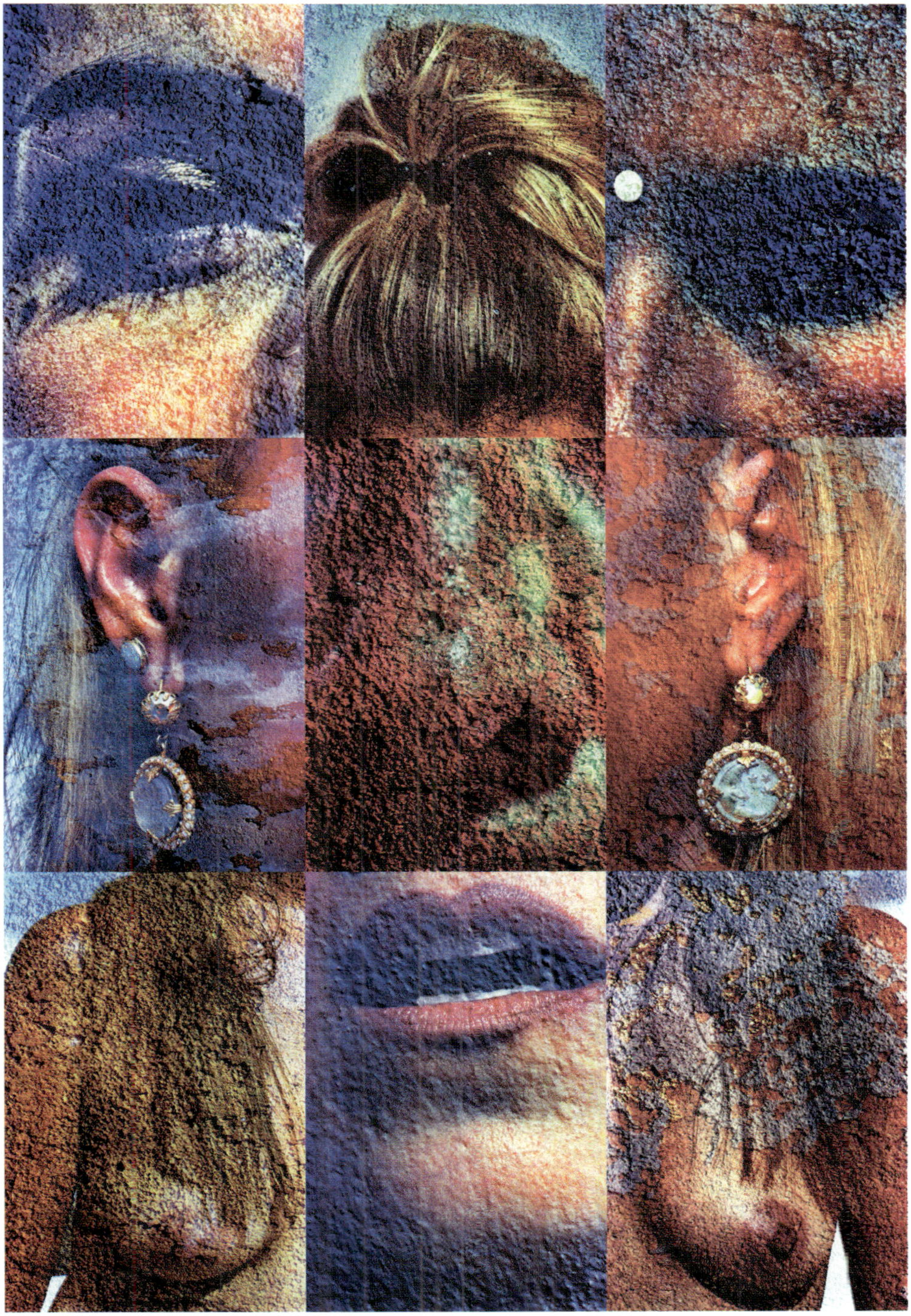

*Three*, 2003.
Nonaptych.

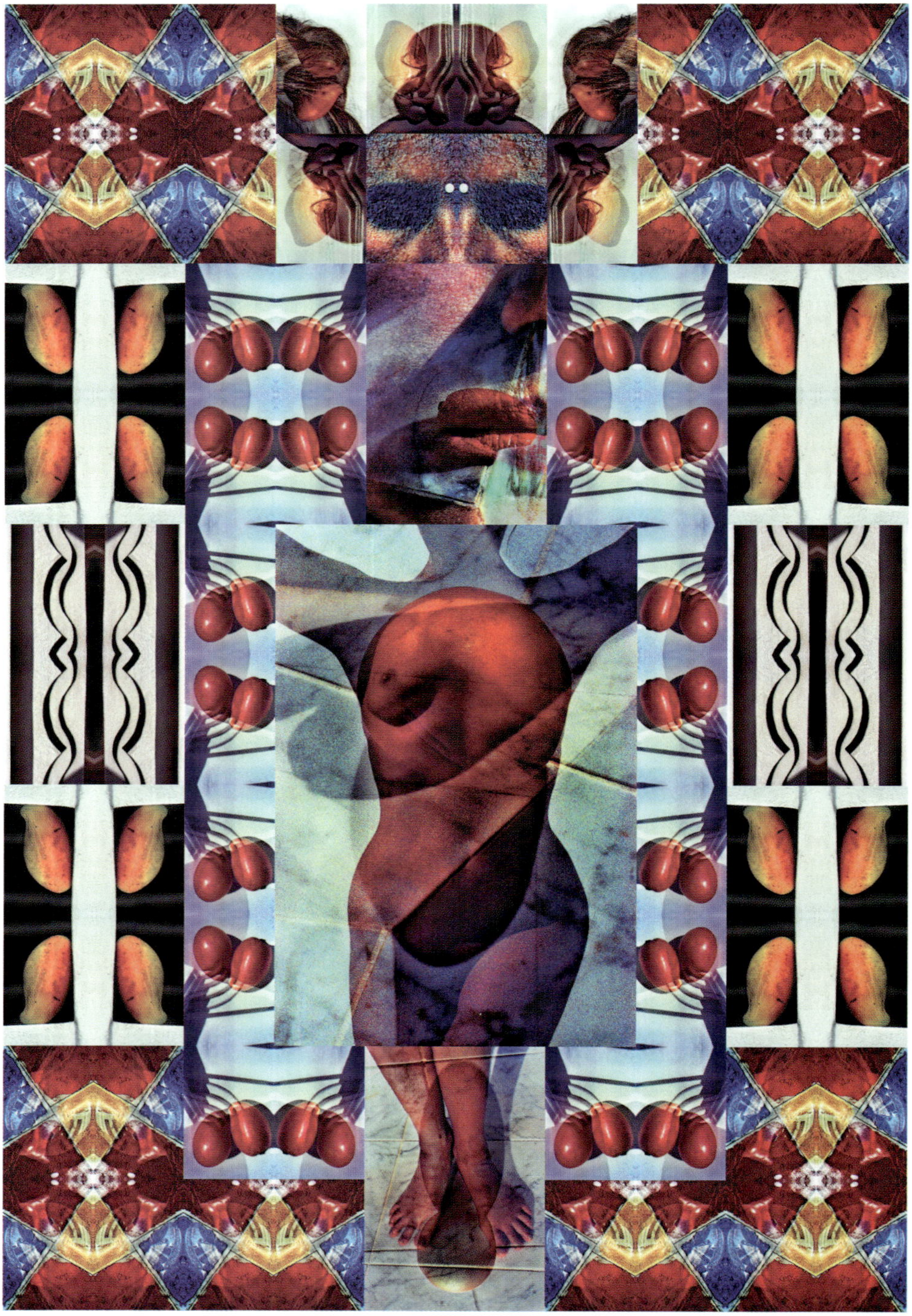

*The Goddess Of Nature Addresses The Two Great Questions Of The "Late-Time"* (detail), 2004.
From *Images 2004*.
Complex Configuration.

During this period, Adi Da moved into a schedule of simultaneous daily configuring and shooting—using the afternoon sun to shoot the pristine beach and building, and the next morning to compose with chips using the new frames. The configurations became elaborate interplays of many subjects. At the culmination of this work, there was barely an inch of space left in Adi Da's studio, with tens of thousands of chips stacked on every flat surface in the room. The title for Adi Da's last elaborate composition of this period points to its paradoxical meaning. He named it, "The Goddess Of Nature Addresses The Two Great Questions Of The 'Late-Time'".

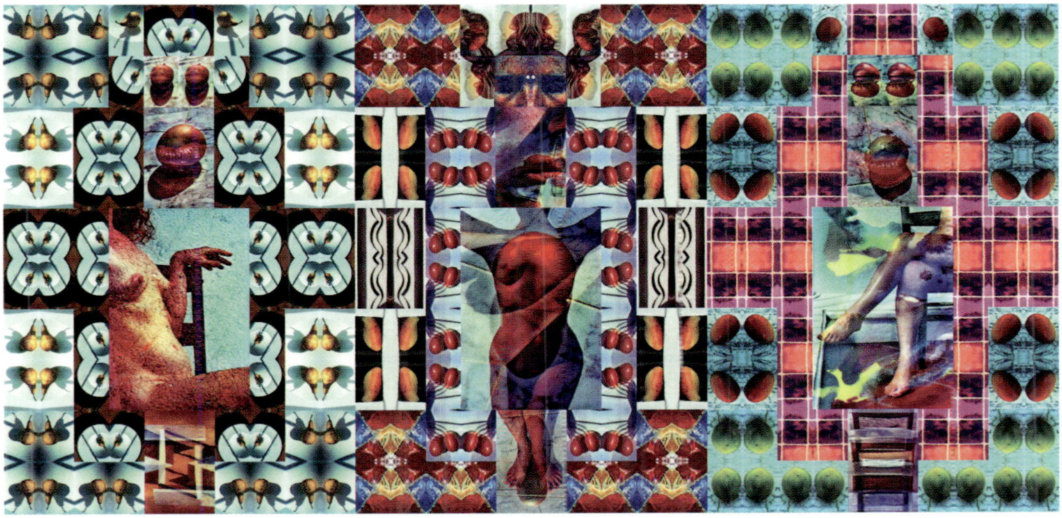

*The Goddess Of Nature Addresses The Two Great Questions Of The "Late-Time"*, 2004.
From *Images 2004.*
Triptych of complex Configurations.

ADI DA SAMRAJ: SUITES OF COMPLEX IMAGE-CONFIGURATIONS
June 2003–February 2004

*The Breather.* 2,662 Image-Configurations.

*Kaleidoscape.* 6,211 Image-Configurations.

*The Spherical Tower.* 3,912 Image-Configurations.

*Three.* 2,787 Image-Configurations.

*Images 2004.* 8,061 Image-Configurations.

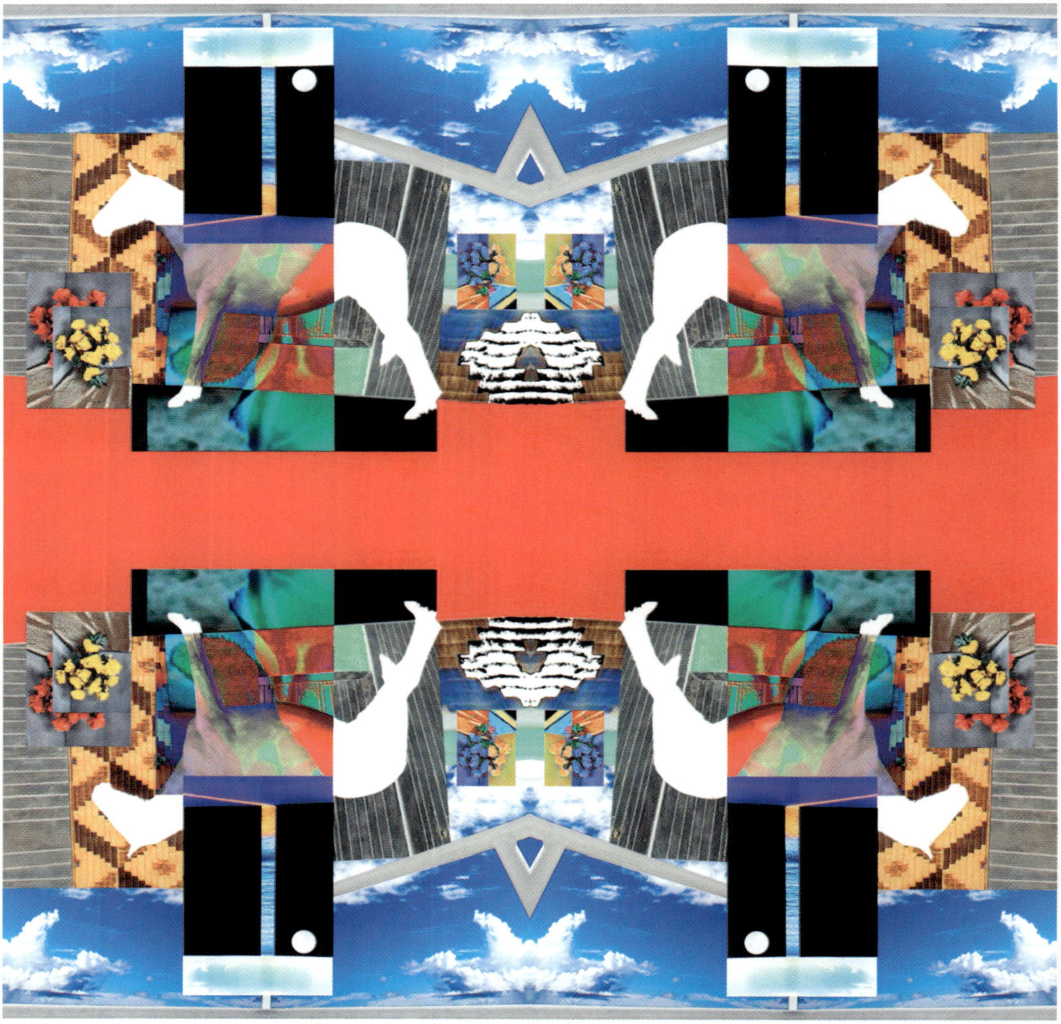

*Spectra Two VIII/7*, 2006.
From *Spectra Two: A Horse Appears In The Wild Is Always Already The Case.*

CHAPTER ELEVEN

# Primal Views: Root-Shape and Root-Color

## A Summary Moment

Over the next two years, Adi Da's artistic process underwent a deep transformative cycle, only to re-emerge in an entirely new form. It was a critical moment in his relationship to his entire—now staggeringly huge—opus of 60,000 works. He reviewed his colossal body of images, along with the entire history of his artistic approach, the progression of his working methods, and every technical means: still cameras, video, sets with projections, and chips for configurations. Once he had surveyed the sum total of his artistry to date, in March of 2006, Adi Da turned to an entirely new medium for his image-making: the tools of digital technology.

This same two-year period in Adi Da's artistic process paralleled a dramatic shift in the field of photography itself, from film to digital cameras. A new level of technology was now available for the first time. Central to Adi Da's interest in the digital medium was his ability to access an unlimited number of images at once. By moving into the digital realm, his oeuvre could be dissolved into one giant resource for the next revolution in his work.

Adi Da compared this turning point in his visual art to the massive burning of all his writings and art in 1965. Suddenly, he was freed from the necessity—and, at this point, the impossibility—of handling the vast quantities of images in physical form. As with the burning of his work forty years before, the dissolution of a massive effort created an internalization of his creative work. Naming the new instantly accessible database his "virtual paintbox", Adi Da had a fresh start for his image-making. Now he had the means to develop "an unlimited visual dictionary" from which to make pictures.

Adi Da's aim, as always, was to reveal reality itself—via abstractions using non-naturalistic colors. For his unique purposes, he found the digital medium could offer him a single method of working. Adi Da envisioned the potential of using digital means to make images that would be even more aesthetically complex than his past work, and that would, in fact, be the fulfillment of the deeply philosophical approach he had been developing since his youth.

# "Responsive Paintbrushes"

Adi Da saw in the digital medium a capacity to "introduce shape, pattern, content, and color into any zone" of an image. He planned to use digital composition like painting, making an entirely original image, rather than replicating imagery from other sources. His one concern, however, was that the demands of the technology would get between him and the subject and obstruct the speed and directness of his working. The challenge was to find a way to work digitally as fluidly as he had worked in the past, just as he had picked up a pen or camera. So, he trained a small group of technicians to handle the software operations while he composed, freeing him from touching the computer. He wanted the technicians to be able to function as extensions of his hands, like "responsive paintbrushes".

Speaking of his digital paintings, Adi Da referred again to his unique understanding of brain processes as a parallel to the aesthetic structures of his images.

*Cézanne and the Impressionists characteristically used short little brushstrokes. My so-called "brushstrokes" are very, very small. They are bytes, pixels—analogous to how the brain organizes and generates visual perception. But the interest I have in the digital process is not merely technical.*

*When I work, I am always standing outside the "seat" of the technology. The interest I have in the technology is strictly in terms of visual or perceptual phenomena, so that I am still working with the fundamentals of perception, rather than getting involved in "techie" business. My intention is to be fully involved in the perceptual process and in the generating of images that perfectly manifest the characteristic of reality itself.*

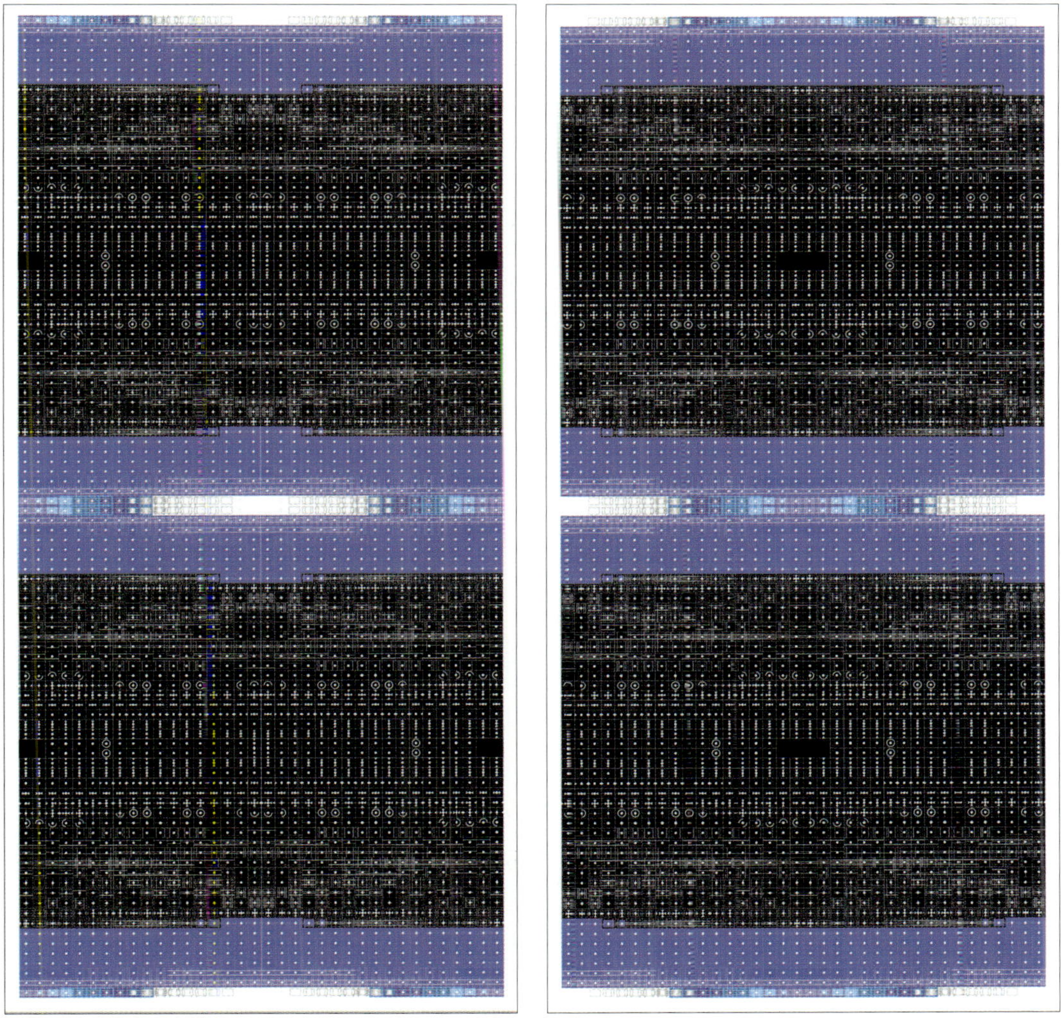

*Twin Towers 2*, 2006.
From *Geome Two: 2001*.

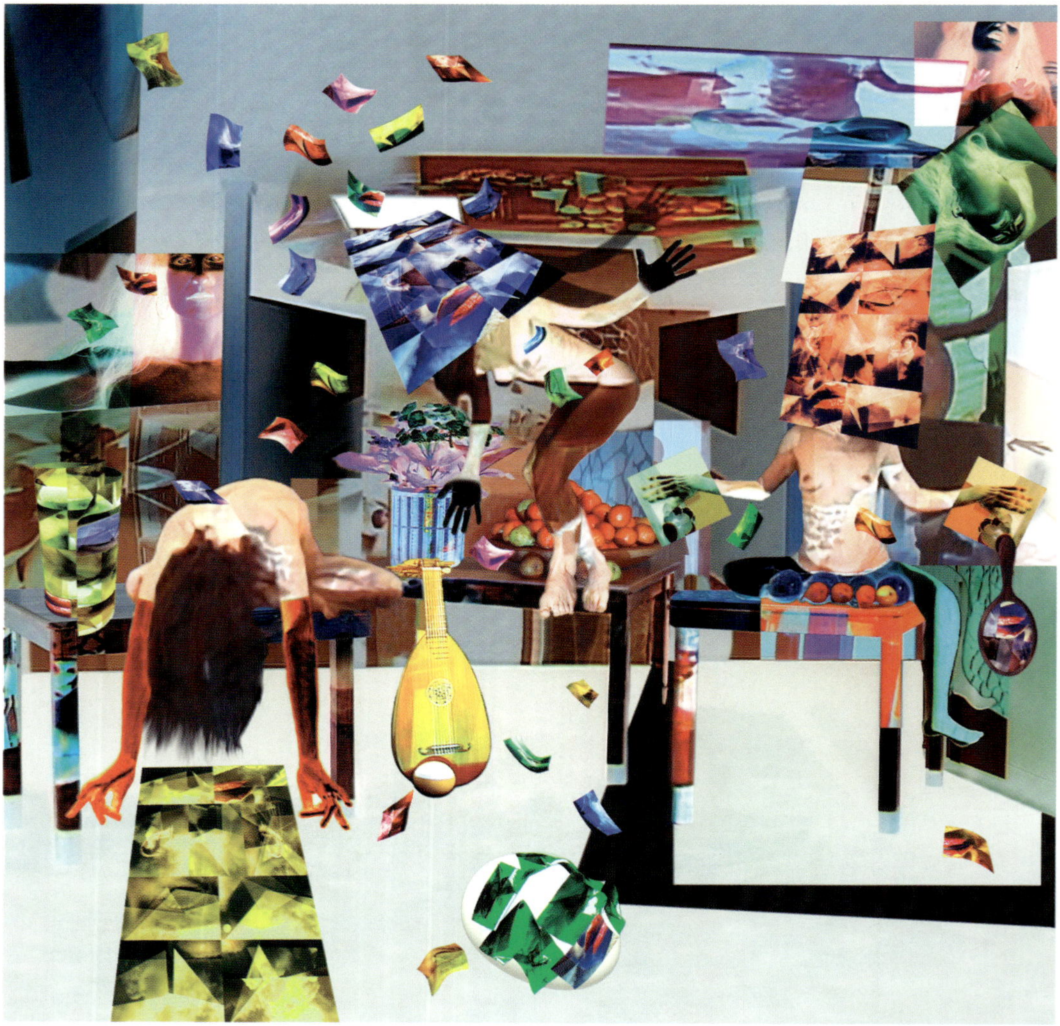

*Spectra One IV/1*, 2006.
From *Spectra One: The Pastimes of Narcissus.*

## The *Spectra* Suites

When Adi Da launched into his digital image-making, the first suite to emerge was his magnificent *Spectra One: The Pastimes of Narcissus*, a highly complex collage with three figures in the "room" of life, showing birth, life, and death. Adi Da began his composition by using video stills from suites he had made in 2001, morphing and fusing the images into hundreds of layers. He was now using images as "virtual chips", without fixed sizes or borders. He compared *Spectra One* to an intricate painting, the entire surface "worked all over", as if in precise layers of oils.

As the name of the *Spectra* suites implies, his communication was about the nature of color, or "manifest light", and also "white light", beyond the prismatic domain. The *Spectra* suites established a new pattern of artistic work for Adi Da—taking a "root-image" and carrying the viewer through a continuum of color values, as the original image is multiplied, mirrored, and magnified.

As a culmination of his working principles, *Spectra* brought Adi Da to an aesthetic refinement in alignment with the deepest meanings of his work. By the end of *Spectra*, "pure" geometry, as well as "pure" color—terms he came to speak and write about at length—had emerged as his main approach to image-making.

Color, in addition to form, holds great meaning for Adi Da. With the digital tools, he developed a highly precise level of color choices. Colors in Adi Da's images are intentionally chosen for their purity and emotional force.

*The colors should be pure colors, not colors that are the product of mixing a particular color with colors other than itself.*

*A pure color is a vibration. It can be measured on a spectral graph. Each color has a certain zone of vibration. I do not merely mix colors on a palette and come up with some different color by mixing yellow and red and green and coming up with something. No, I use only pure colors, a piece of the spectrum of visible light. That is the idea of* Spectra.

*Color is not arbitrary. It must be exactly right for each image in particular.*

*Color has emotional force. Colors in relation to one another generate, by that relatedness, different modes, or tones, of emotional force.*

*Color has meaning in the nervous system, in the folds of the brain. That meaning is not something that can altogether be stated verbally, but meaning is inherent in color.*

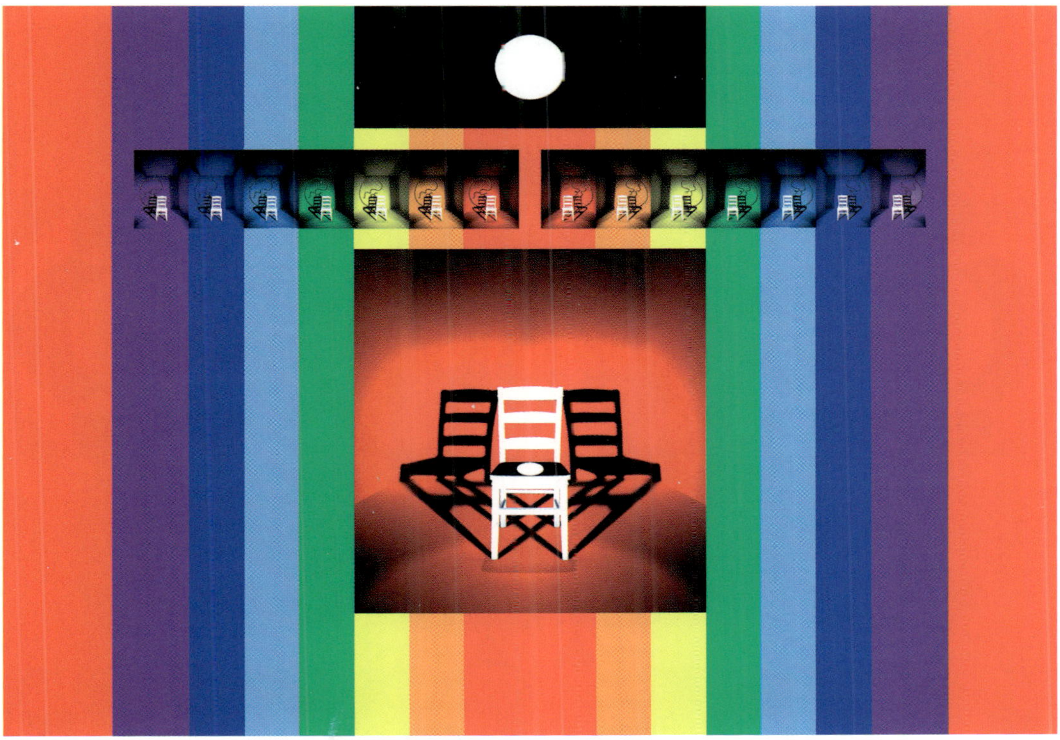

*Spectra Nine I/1*, 2006.
From *Spectra Nine: The Autobiography of Everybody*.

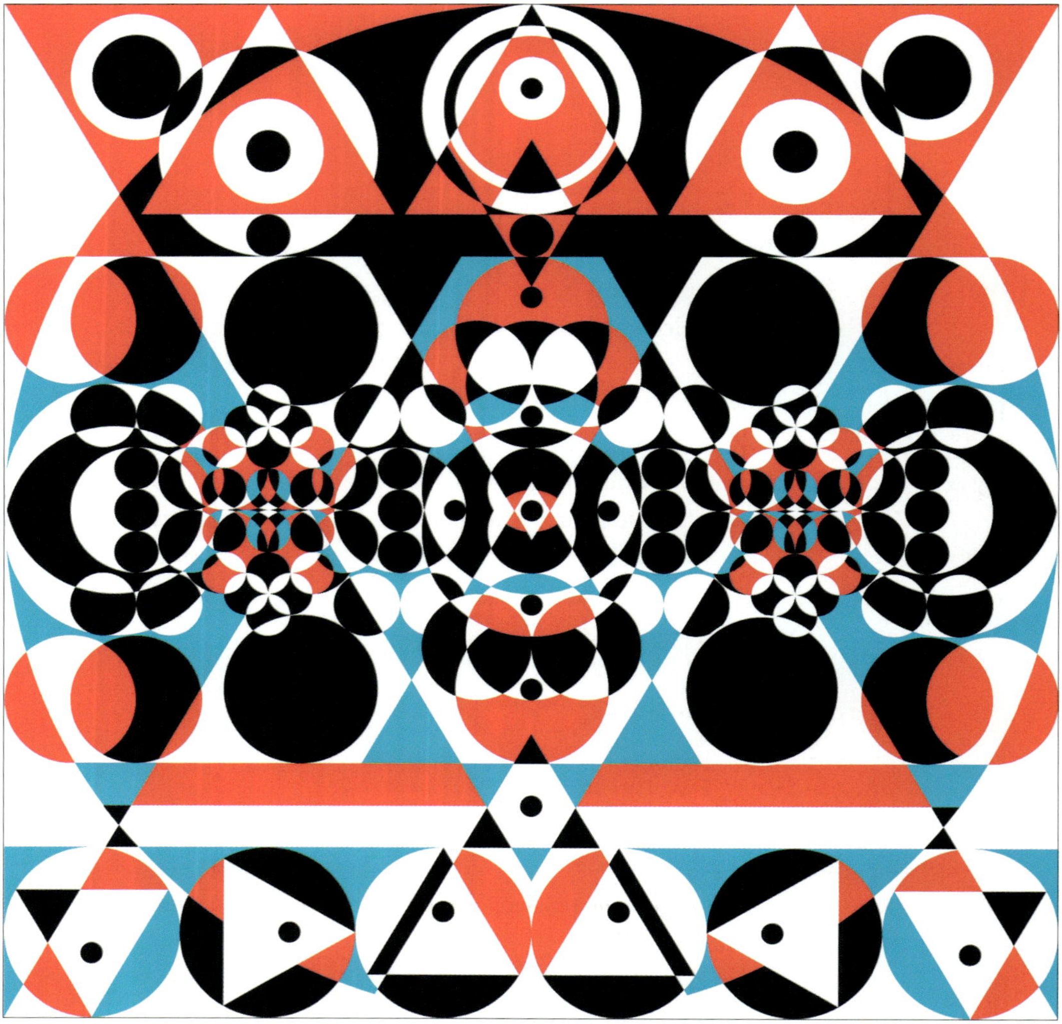

*She (The Transcendental State Of The Nude Subject) 7*, 2006.
From *Geome Four: The Subject In Question.*

# The *Geome* Suites

The *Geome* suites premiered Adi Da's virtuoso work with squares, circles, and triangles in the radiant colors of his new palette. The structure of this work was a kind of "epitome" of all his development to this point, the digital means now providing the capacity for precision in depicting what Adi Da identified as the primary form of the universe, geometry itself.

Geometry had been of great importance to Adi Da's artistic development since he was a child. Growing up in a small town in the 1940s, Adi Da credits an early television show, "Learning to Draw with Jon Gnagy", as his first course in the principles of modern art. Gnagy was popularizing the principles of Cézanne by showing how any picture can be made up of basic shapes. Adi Da took this discussion of geometry to another level, via his interest in the "structures of perception".

Adi Da summarizes this idea as "the natural world of primary shape", saying that it is possible to become aware of the manifest universe as being actually constructed of these primary geometric forms, if one is available to the deepest levels of awareness.

*The force of primary geometric forms is everywhere in the world. It is simply that there are so many intersections of primary geometric form in ordinary perceived reality that it feels as if you cannot see the primary form. It is not that perceived reality is made out of "four circles" and "three rectangles" and "two triangles"—you cannot see the world that simplistically. But, once you begin to "get" the sense of "shape", then you can see that the world of perception is actually made of primary geometries. It is just that there are so many of them all at once that the natural world seems to have "feathered edges". The natural world does not seem to be hard-edged, in terms of geometry. In fact, the natural world is <u>not</u> visibly hard-edged—when the multiples are in the billions, trillions, countless numbers all at once. Then the world of perception has the kind of "feathered edges" you apparently see in the natural world.*

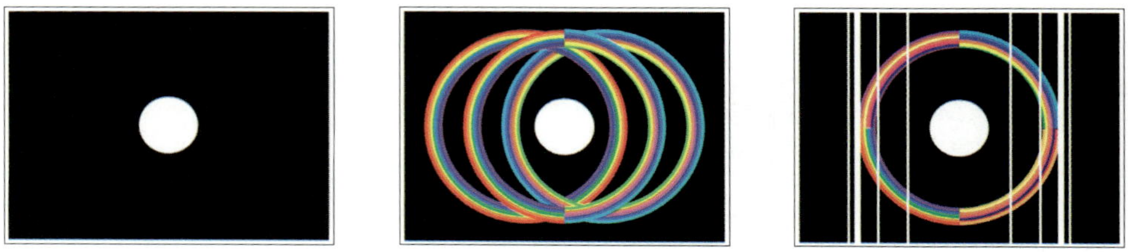

*Thus, the basis of the natural world's construction is primary shape, primary geometry, elemental shape—circular, linear, angular. Everything is one of those three—curved, strictly linear, or angled. The intersection of these three modes of geometry makes virtually every shape. If you take enough triangles, squares, and circles, any form will appear. You put them together in certain conjunctions, and they will make absolutely every form.*

*The image-art I create takes as its "starting point" the world as it seems to be—which is multiples of primary geometries, intersecting with each other many, many times, such that the perceptible form seems to be soft-edged.*

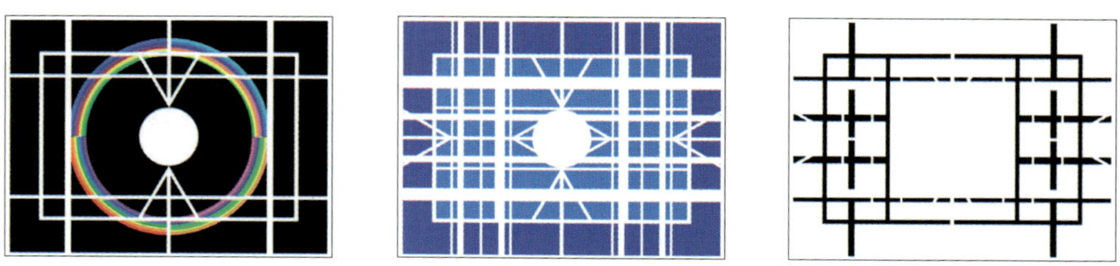

*What Is Not An Idea?*, 2006. Six Images.
From *Geome Two: 2001*.

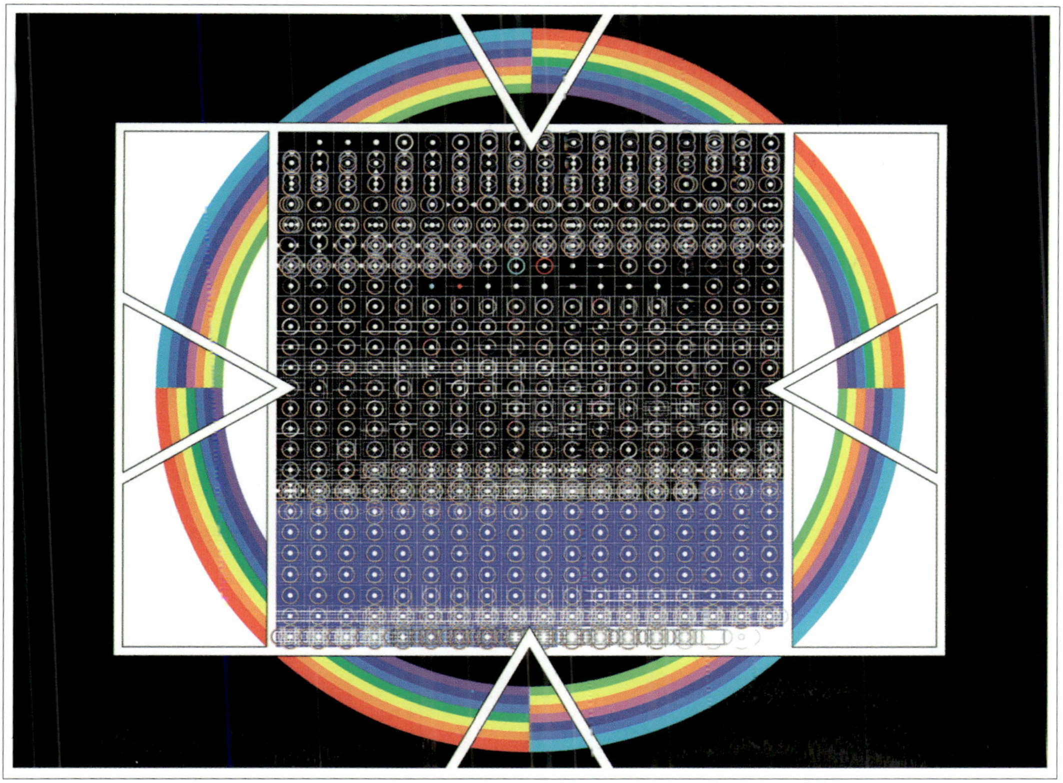

*First Sighting 39*, 2006.
From *Geome Twc: 2001*.

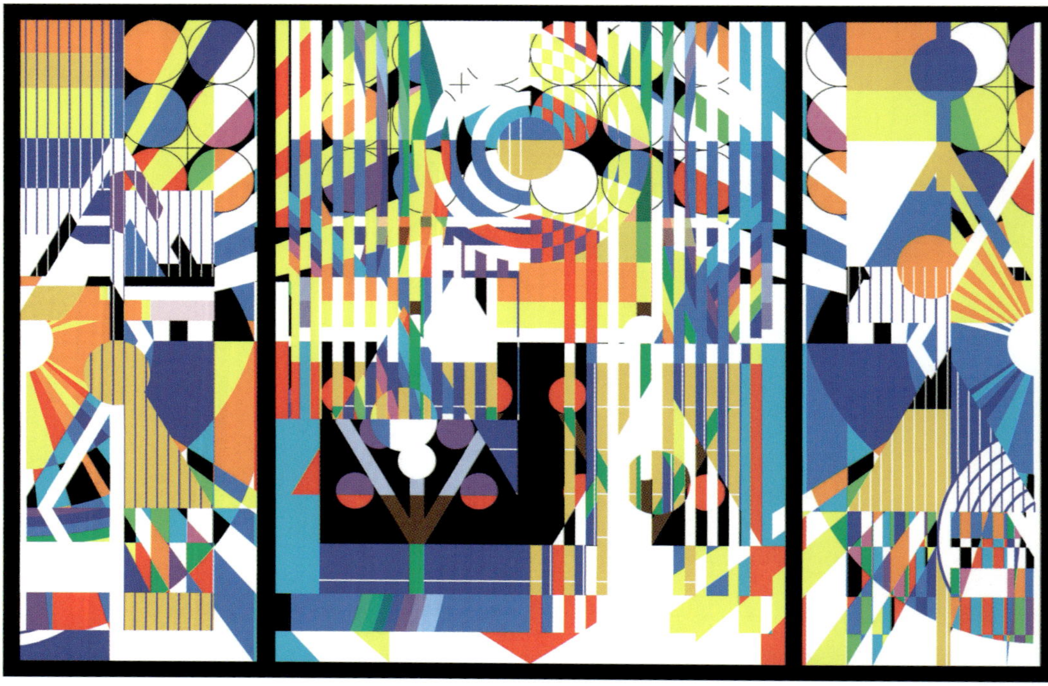

*The Order Of The Day: Tuesday 7*, 2006.
From *Geome One: Alberti's Window*.

# A New Working Process

In the making of the *Geome* suites, Adi Da came to a new system of working, in keeping with his principle of relationship to the subject—this time, using the digital medium's capacity for unlimited abstraction and razor-like precision. Once again, he used photography to create a source-image. But often, rather than work "on top of" the photograph, he would gaze upon it as a kind of recorded inspiration, likening it to a sketchpad. The photograph might sit to his side as he, in response to it, placed precise lines, circles, and colors on the digital screen, abstracting the subject into geometries on the spot. This first-generation image still retains recognizable references to the original "natural" subject.

What happens next in Adi Da's current creation of images is quite intriguing. Once he completes the first abstraction from the photograph into geometries, this image itself becomes the new subject for his response. As Adi Da explained, "The images I have made will become the subject, rather than the natural, perceived events with which the process began." Thus, every subsequent image is a further abstraction. Nevertheless, he always maintains a "continuing association" with the perceptual events and places that are his subjects.

As Adi Da pointed out, this kind of progressive abstraction has been a characteristic of his aesthetic process all along. What he found now, however, was a "level of resolution and complexity" that afforded him the ability to respond to the subject and then "modify freely" in response to the abstractions themselves.

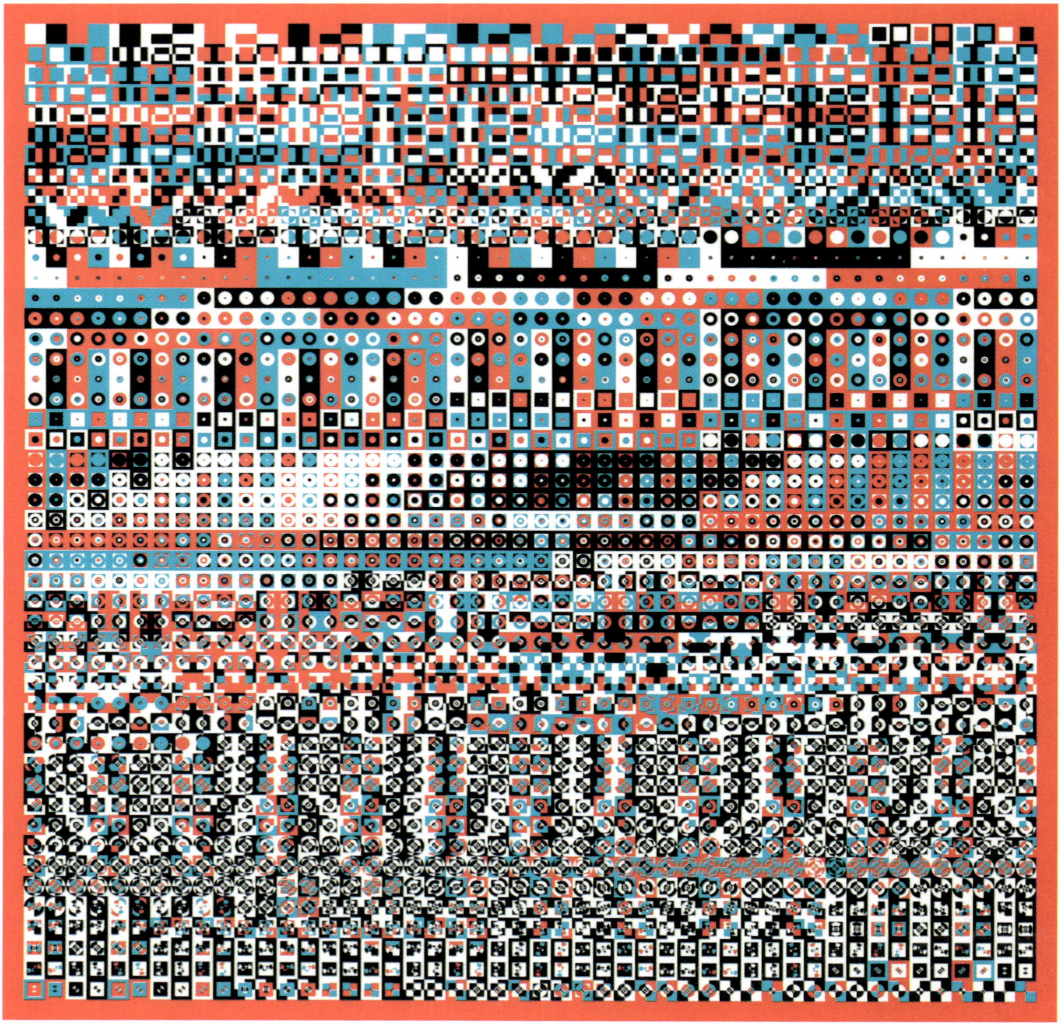

*NYCSTET VI*, 2006.
From *Geome Three: The Scale of Perfection*.

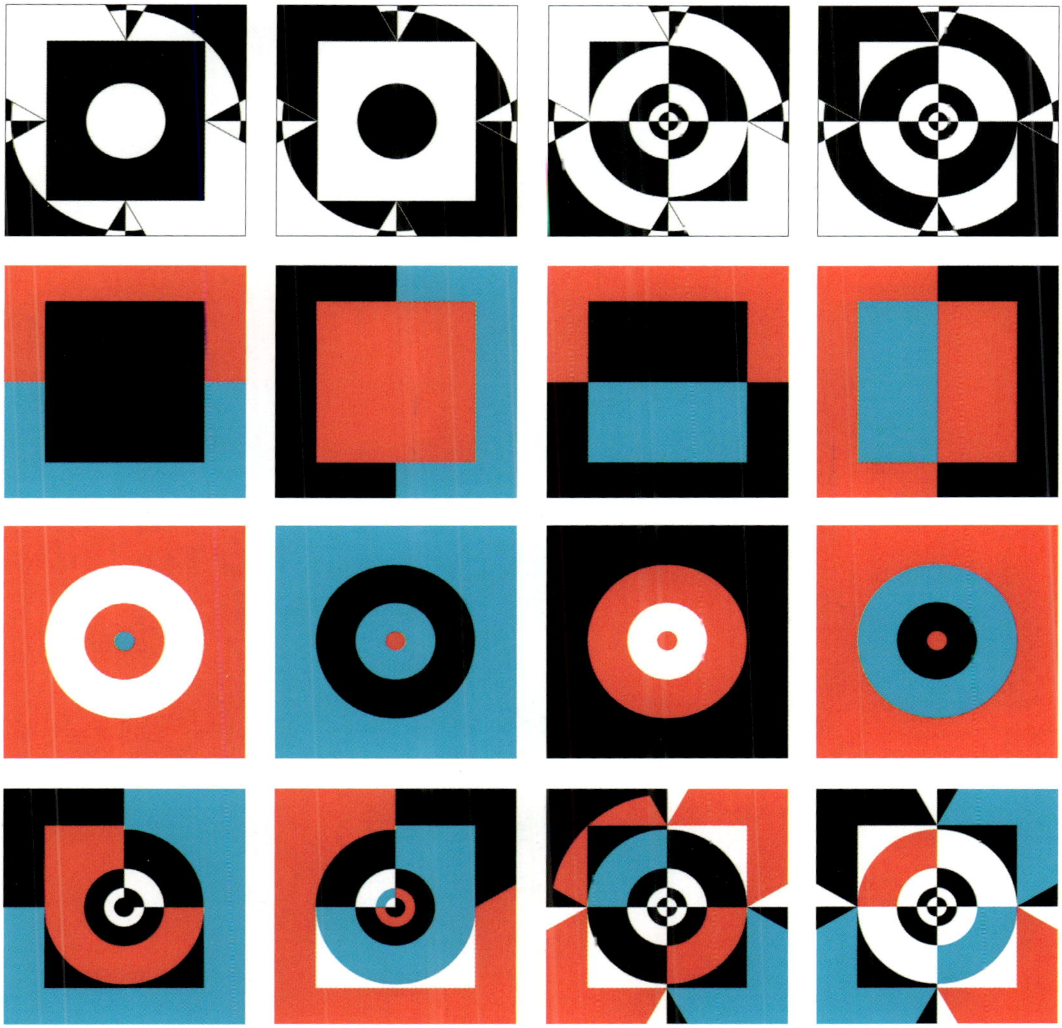

*Perfect Circles,* 2006. Four Images (top line).
*Perfect Squares, 2006.* Twelve Images (remaining three lines).
From *Geome Three: The Scale of Perfection.*

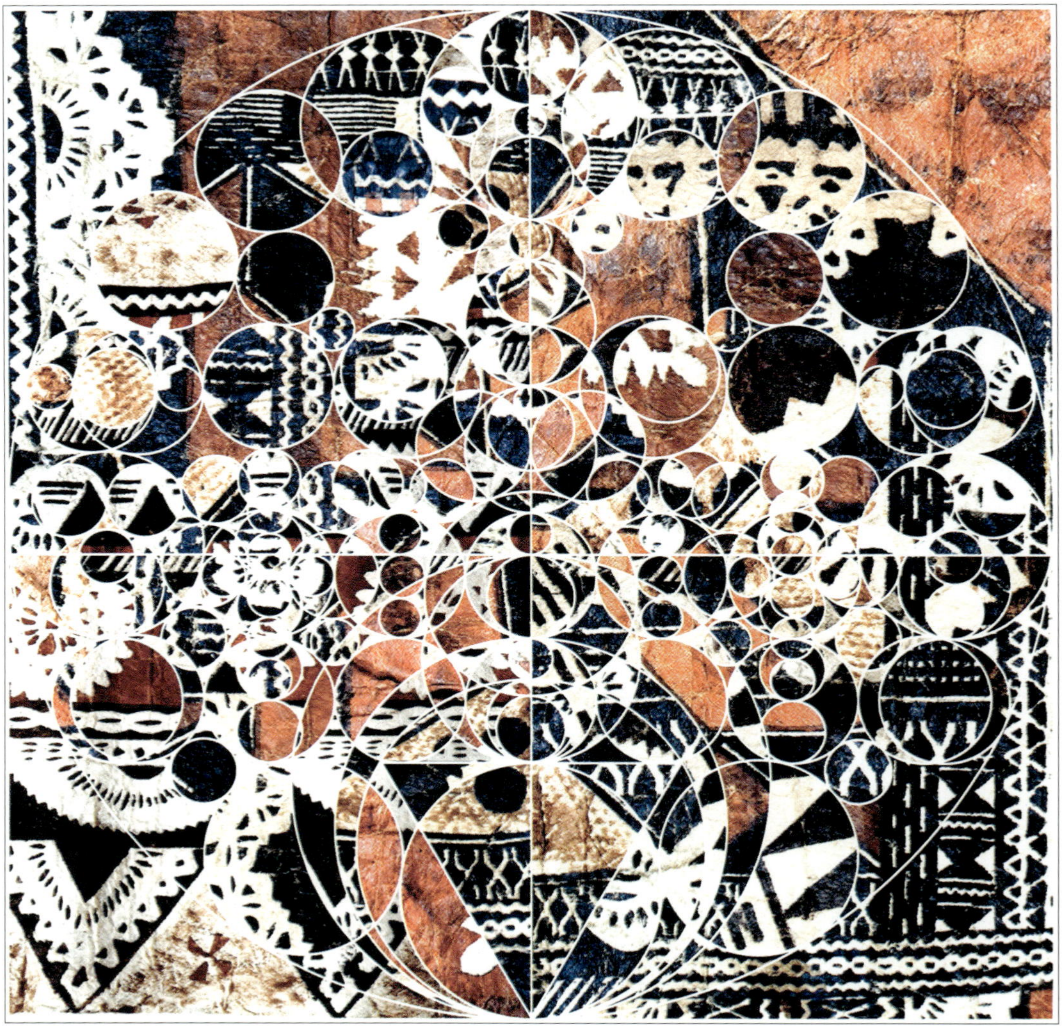

*Ciqomi Women III/2*, 2006.
From *Geome Five: Ciqomi (Acception), Acception IV: The Women Of Ciqomi*.

A composite of photographs of Fijian decorated bark-cloth (tapa).
"Ciqomi"—a Fijian word meaning "reception", or "acception"—is the name of a village on the island where Adi Da resides in Fiji. ("Ciqomi" is pronounced "thing-go-mee".)

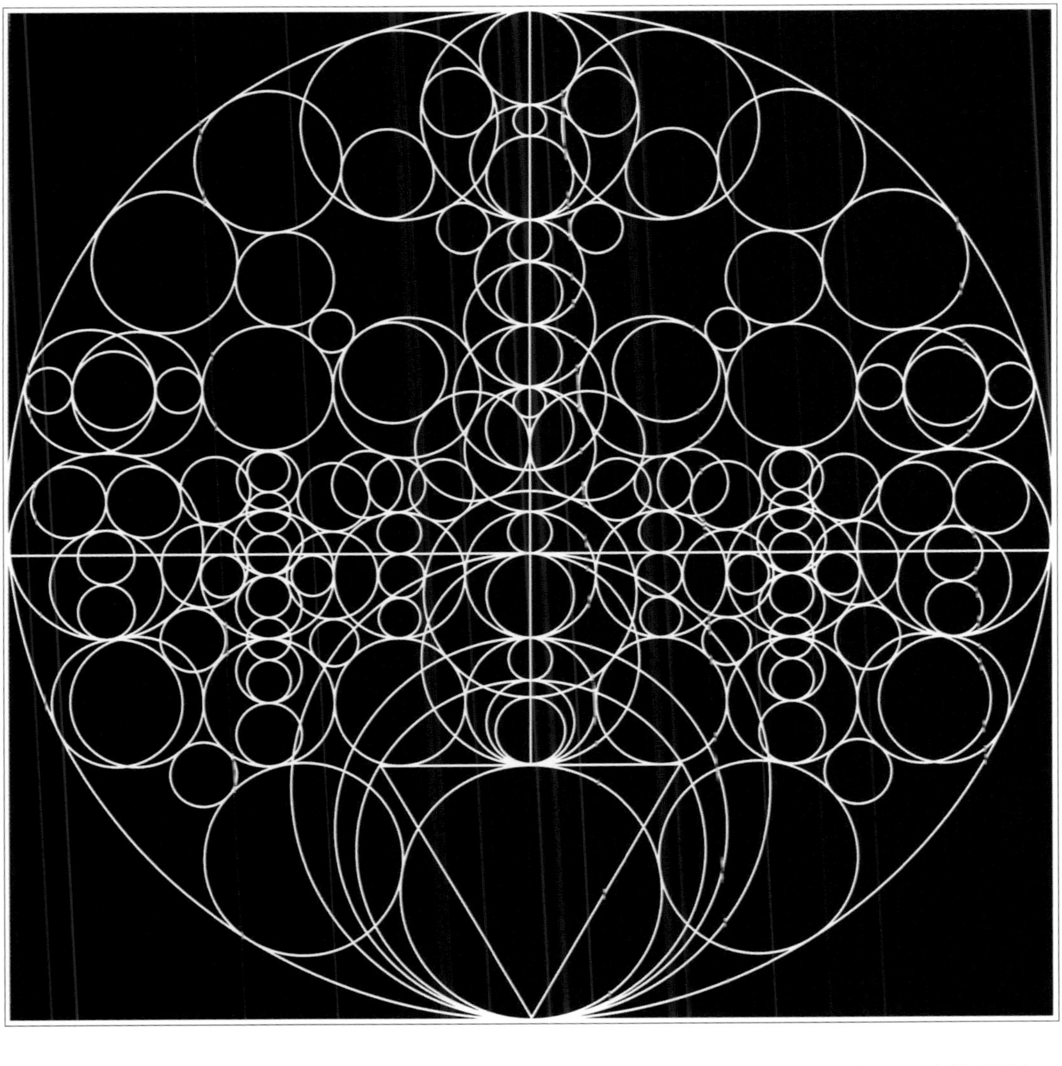

*Ciqomi Women IV/2*, 2006.
From *Geome Five: Ciqomi (Acception), Acception IV: The Women Of Ciqomi.*

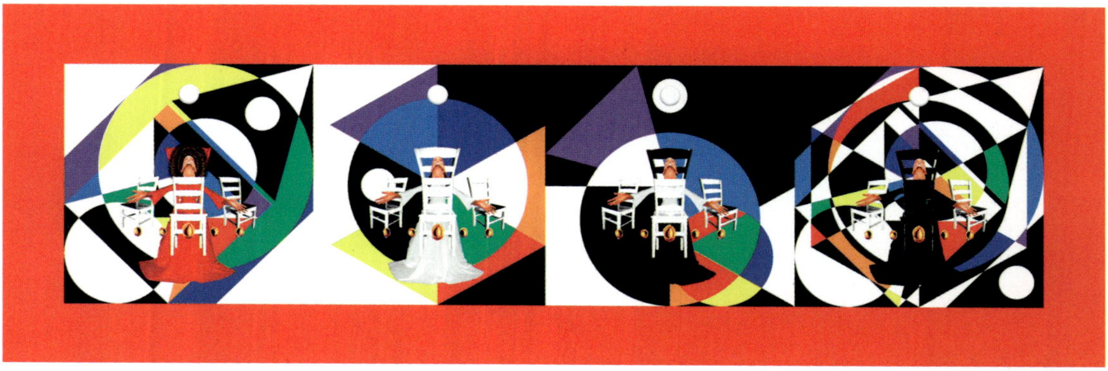

*The Reduction Of The Beloved To Love Alone—Part One/1a, 2006.*
From *Oculus One: The Reduction Of The Beloved.*

## The Beginning of *Oculus*

In the *Oculus* suites, still in progress at the time of this writing, Adi Da returns to his work with the female form, now in his language of geometric abstraction and intense, vibratory colors. The oculus—meaning "an eyelike or round window, often appearing at the height of a dome"—appears as a white sphere in the top of the imagery. Like the ceiling hole, the "midnight sun", and the "hole in the universe" in his earlier work, Adi Da's oculus is the opening to spiritual revelation, to the light beyond the "room" of the apparent world.

The subtitle of *Oculus One—The Reduction Of The Beloved*—is a direct reference to Adi Da's thesis on modernism from his graduate studies (*The Reduction Of The Beloved To Shape Alone*). And, indeed, in *Oculus*, he restores abstraction to its original, liberating purpose.

Adi Da said of this suite:

*The female figure in* Oculus One *can be seen to be the beloved—in a progress from lover to bride to wife to widow—who is being "reduced" by that process, and also reduced to love itself, or to loving while being alone. It also can be understood that "the beloved" is not that figure, but that the female figure is relating to one beloved to her.*

*There is nothing necessarily negative implied in the title* The Reduction Of The Beloved To Love Alone. *There is a kind of realization in that, rather than loss—though there is also a suggestion of loss, being alone. All such meanings are intended, and are there to be felt.*

*The forms of the lover, the bride, the wife, and the widow show the same attitude—the same ecstatic, contemplative head and figure altogether. The same posture is the sign of all the figures, but each has unique iconographic attributes. There are differences in the breast forms, in the hair, in the color of the chairs. For instance, the wife figure has a combined black and white chair. One foot in bed and one foot in the grave. In other words, the wife form is in between life and death, participating in both. The breasts are down-pointing—suggesting perhaps the nursing of a child, without having a child in the image. There is no wild hair—the hair is pulled back. Hair suggests the characteristic of orientation to sexuality and life-energy. So the wife shows more maturity, more age, and so forth. And yet, it is still the same attitude and state as the other female figures.*

*In the widow form, the background is a kind of collision between all the previous ones. It is a shattered structure. The widow is a kind of shattered structure in the black form. Yet the widow form has the same attitude, the same disposition, the same contemplative and surrendered disposition that is characteristic of all the forms of the figure in this suite. So the differences are in the mode of how the life-characteristics are shown outwardly. The disposition otherwise shows steadiness—a continuously ecstatic, contemplative, and surrendered disposition, surrendered to what is above and what is beyond. This feminine figure is not affected by life-changes. It is always in the same disposition and surrendered in the context of life-changes.*

*These are not ironic images, nor mere conventional realism in showing the changing female form. There is perhaps something comic about them, but only in the sense that there is something comic about the human process itself. They are a reflection of how the natural process happens and how life-stages happen, and a communication of unaffectedness and surrender, serenity, contemplation.*

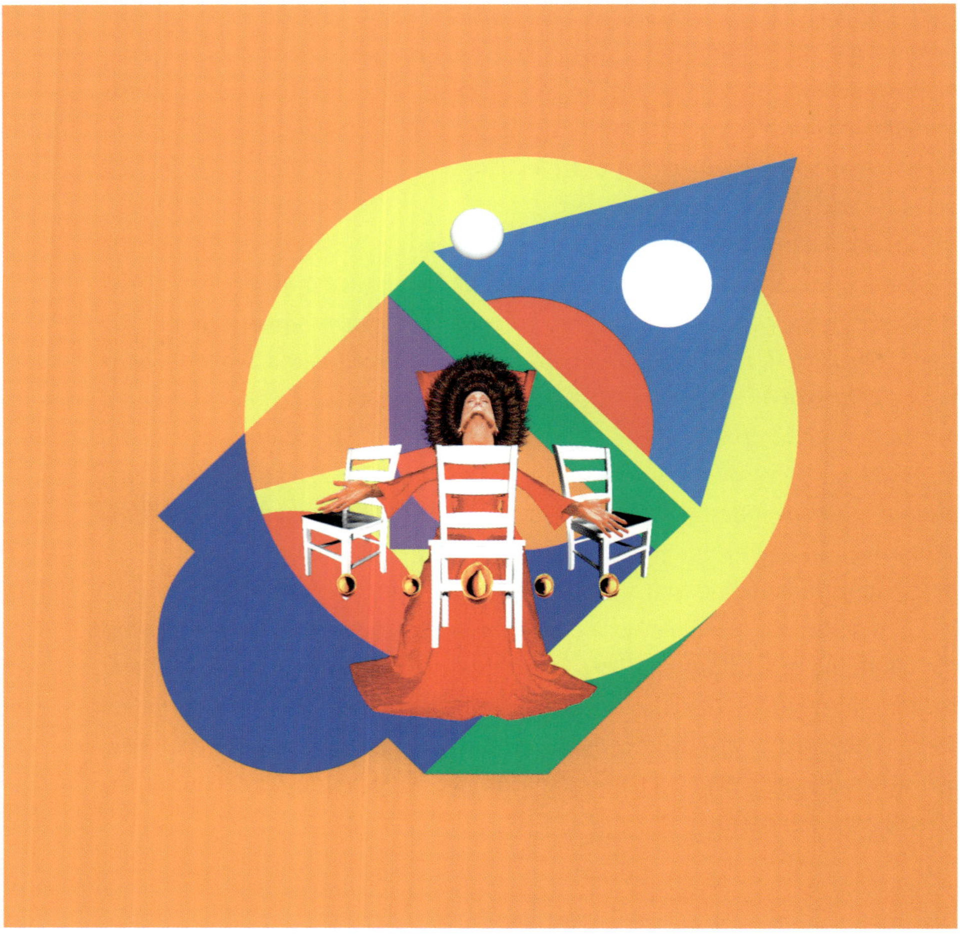

*The Reduction Of The Beloved To Love Alone*—Part Five, *The Lover/3a*, 2006.
From *Oculus One*: *The Reduction Of The Beloved*.

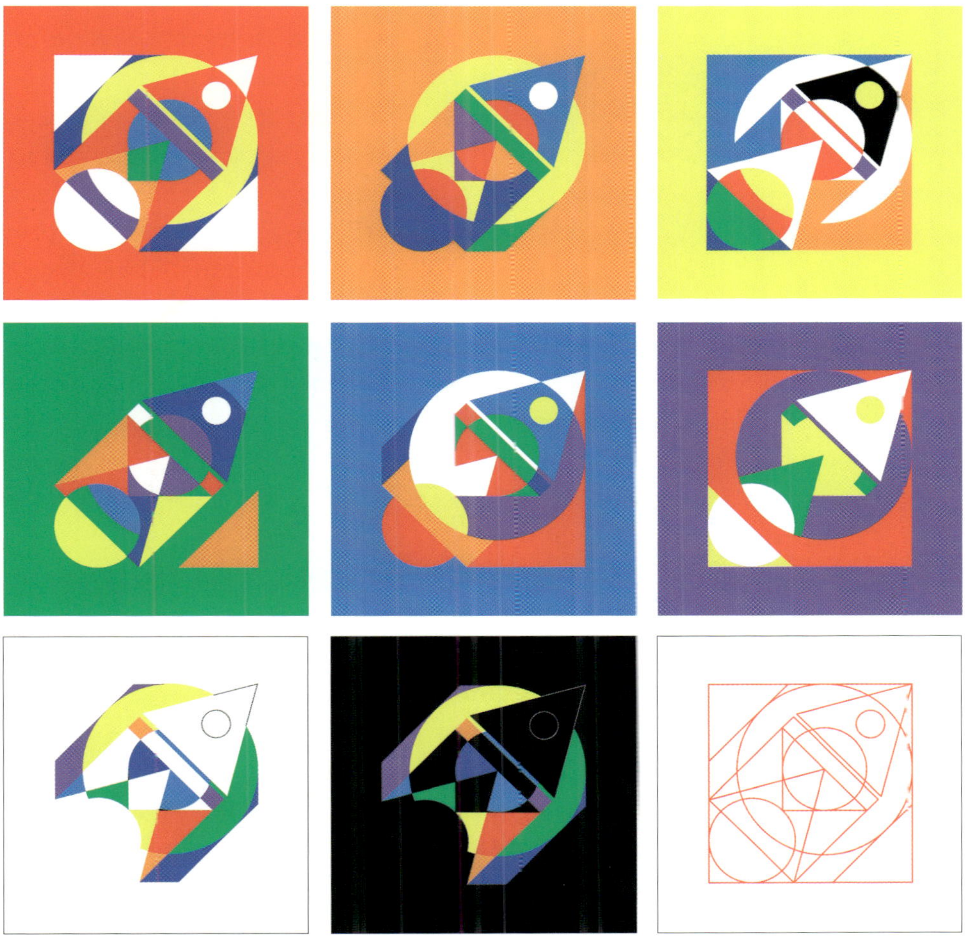

*The Reduction Of The Beloved To As Is*—Part Four, *The Lover*, 2006. Nine Images.
From *Oculus One: The Reduction Of The Beloved*.

# Complex Works of Unity

With *Spectra*, *Geome*, and *Oculus*, Adi Da has come to a profoundly wrought artistic process, the summation of decades of arduous effort. Like his first "encoded artifacts", the many levels of meaning in each image, in the suites, and in his body of work as a whole are held in the structure of the aesthetics. Like the weaver of an infinite and never-ending tapestry, Adi Da works the whole while constantly refining the threads, with the work becoming ever more expansive and opulent.

Key to this process are the components of the suites. In his newest work, Adi Da uses small compositional units of color and form. Like his mosaic-like "complex configurations", his current suites evolve from "root-images", multiplied to infinite combinations. In his *Geome* suites, for example, Adi Da drove his ability to make intricately massive macro-micro relationships within an oeuvre to a new level. Like a galaxy-sized microscope, progressively zooming from a DNA helix out to the Milky Way, Adi Da uses his suites to expand the viewer beyond "point of view" with systematic variations of scale. The incremental variations are the true meaning of the work: to show the "room" as if from every possible "point of view".

In his essay on Adi Da's work for the catalog of the 52nd Biennale di Venezia, Achille Bonito Oliva wrote:

*Adi Da Samraj has established a new use of geometry, as a fertile field of unconventional aesthetic communication that takes delight in developing its principles asymmetrically, through surprise and feeling. However, there is no contradiction between these two elements and the principles of design. Rather, surprise and feeling strengthen those principles, through a pragmatic and un-preconceived use of "representational" geometry. . . .*

*The final form—whether two-dimensional or three-dimensional—suggests a tangible rather than an abstract reality, which pulsates before the thrilled analytical gaze of the beholder.*

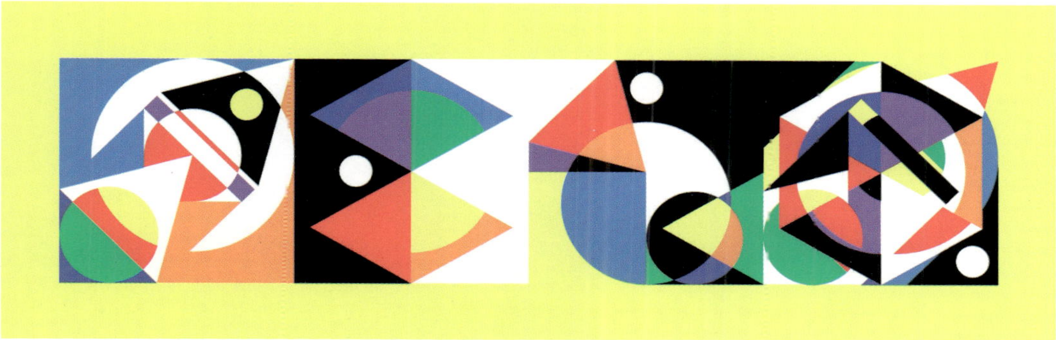

*The Reduction Of The Beloved To As Is*—Part One/4, 2006.
From *Oculus One: The Reduction Of The Beloved.*

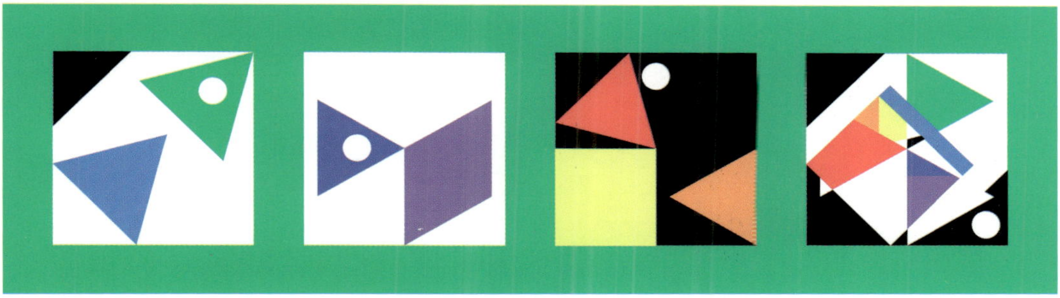

*The Reduction Of The Beloved To As Is*—Part Three, *The Bride/3a*, 2006.
From *Oculus One: The Reduction Of The Beloved.*

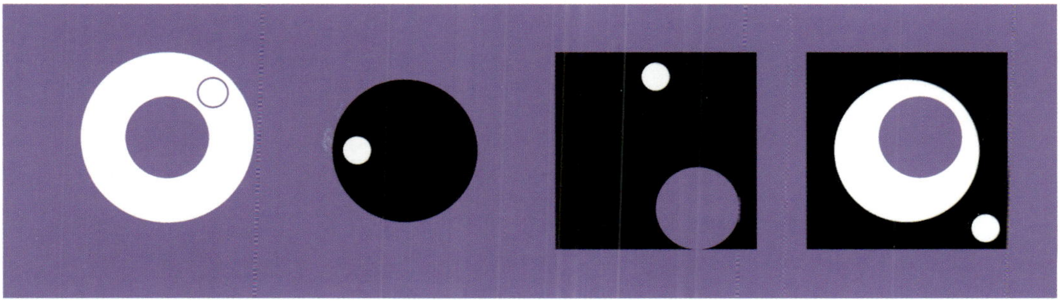

*The Reduction Of The Beloved To As Is*—Part Three, *The Widow/5d*, 2006.
From *Oculus One: The Reduction Of The Beloved.*

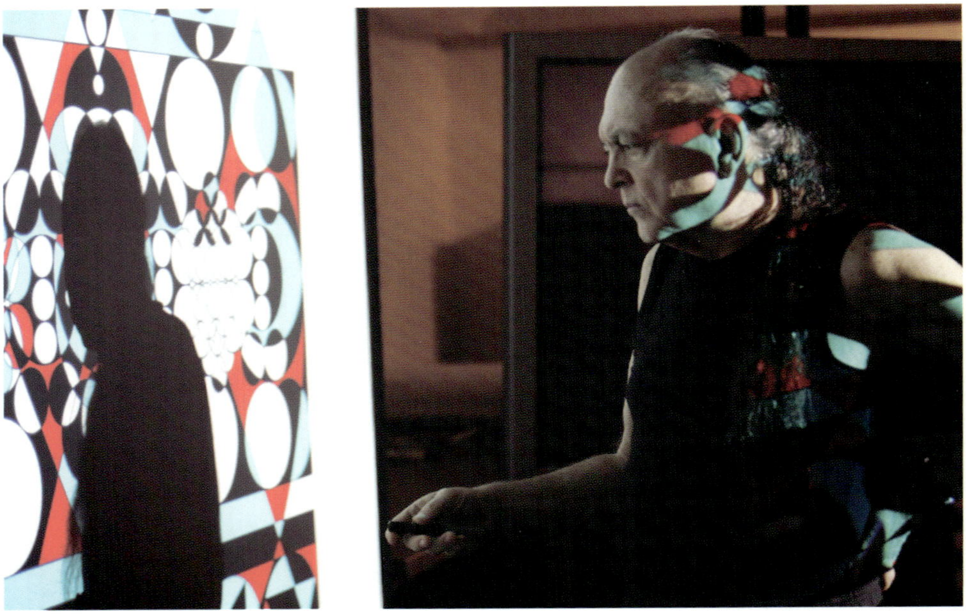

Adi Da Samraj in his studio, during the creation of *Geome Four*.

## The Solitary Room

This is the circumstance in which Adi Da's newest opus arises: In a small thatched building on his island-retreat in Fiji, Adi Da devotes himself to his image-work in his digital studio. Spending many hours a day in front of a large screen, Adi Da gives instructions to the nearby computer assistants, using a laser to pinpoint the locations of lines, colors, and forms as he speaks.

As Adi Da's work continues, his room is increasingly silent, hours going by as he makes the subtlest changes in an image. In this pristine and highly refined environment, Adi Da focuses on his artistic work day in and day out, and on the most minute of details. In this manner, the color and shape of the images are more and more finely aligned. The movements of the laser pointer become smaller, his voice, softer. Adi Da is deep in his work.

## ADI DA SAMRAJ: DIGITALLY-CONSTRUCTED SUITES

April–November 2006

*SPECTRA* SUITES

*Spectra One: The Pastimes of Narcissus.* 103 Images.

*Spectra Two: A Horse Appears In The Wild Is Always Already The Case.* 475 Images.

*Spectra Three: Quandra Contemplating the Fruits of Perfect Knowledge.* 107 Images.

*Spectra Four: The Room Itself Is The Only Witness To The Three Common States.* 189 Images.

*Spectra Five: Not-Two Is Peace.* 48 Images.

*Spectra Six: Not-Two Is Not Two.* 24 Images.

*Spectra Seven: The Self-Portrait.* 24 Images.

*Spectra Eight: Life Is The Perfect Reflection Of Its Source.* 37 Images.

*Spectra Nine: The Autobiography Of Everybody.* 75 Images.

*Spectra Ten: The "First Room" Trilogy.* 126 Images.

*THE PERFECT MIRROR* SUITES

*The Perfect Mirror One: The Voyage.* 87 Images.

*The Perfect Mirror Two: This Is Not-An-Object.* 69 Images.

*The Perfect Mirror Three: Portrait Of The Artist As Not-An-Object.* 11 Images.

*GEOME* SUITES

*Geome One: Alberti's Window.* 1,416 Images.

*Geome Two: 2001.* 1,101 Images.

*Geome Three: The Scale Of Perfection.* 5,454 Images.

*Geome Four: The Subject In Question.* 354 Images.

*Geome Five: Ciqomi (Acception).* 833 Images.

*OCULUS* SUITES

*Oculus One: The Reduction Of The Beloved.* 2,644 Images.

Further *Oculus* Suites are in progress as of the publication of this book.

# The Unobservable Totality of Light

## An Epilogue in the Words and Pictures of Adi Da Samraj

*The irreducible paradox of unobservability and unknowability is the actual real state of every one and every thing.*

All quotations in the Epilogue are from "The Unobservable Totality of Light", in *Transcendental Realism: The Image-Art of egoless Coincidence With Reality Itself*, by Adi Da Samraj (Middletown, CA: The Dawn Horse Press, 2007).

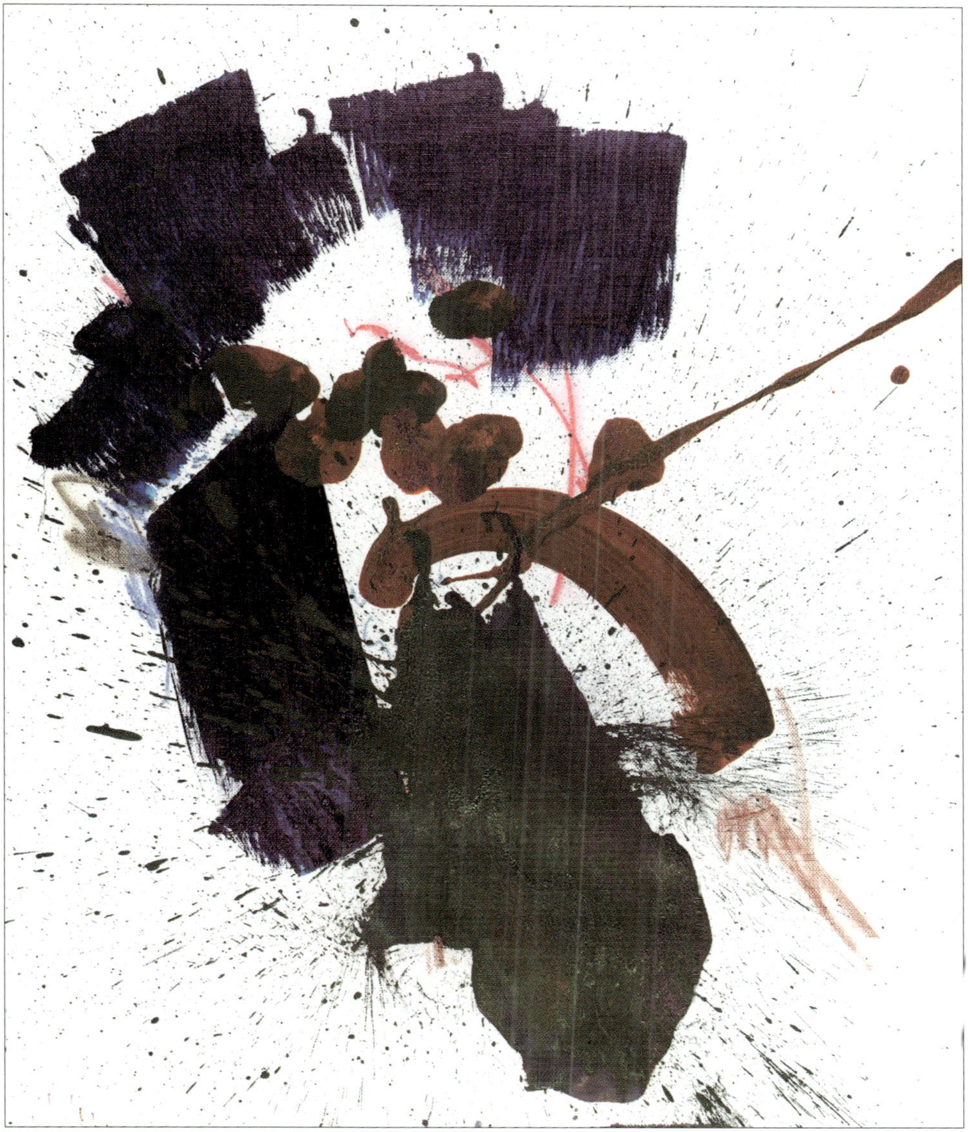

"She" Painting, 1994.
Liquid acrylic paint and oilbar on paper.

*The living body always wants, with wanting need,
to allow the light of perfect reality into the "room".*

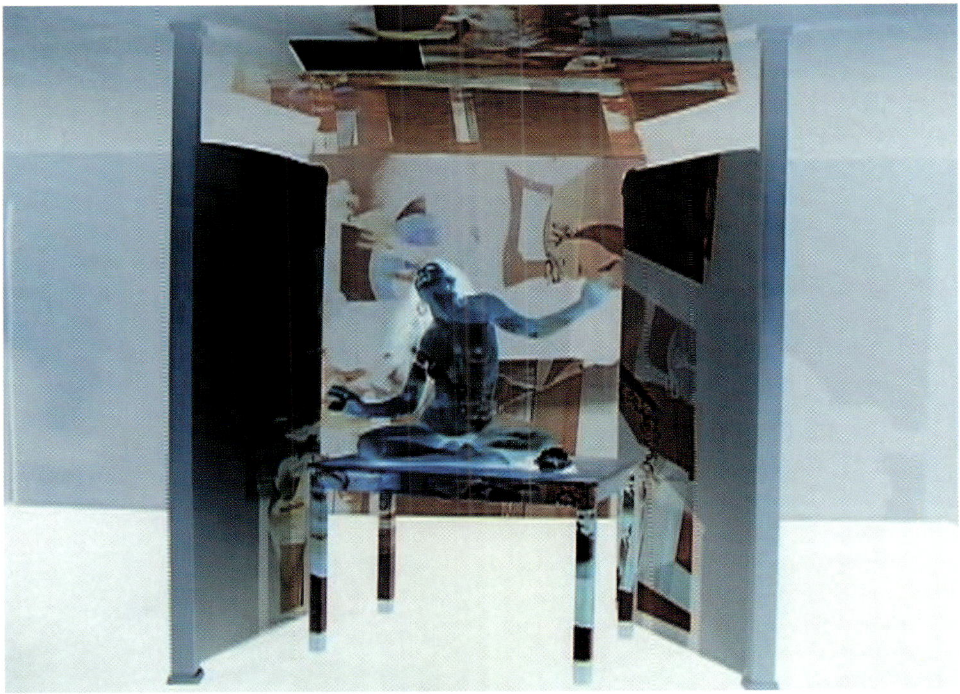

*The Accident of Beauty*, 2001.
Video still.

*Reality has no "thing" in it, no "other" in it, no separate "self" in it, no ideas, no constructs in mind or perception, and, altogether, no "point of view".*

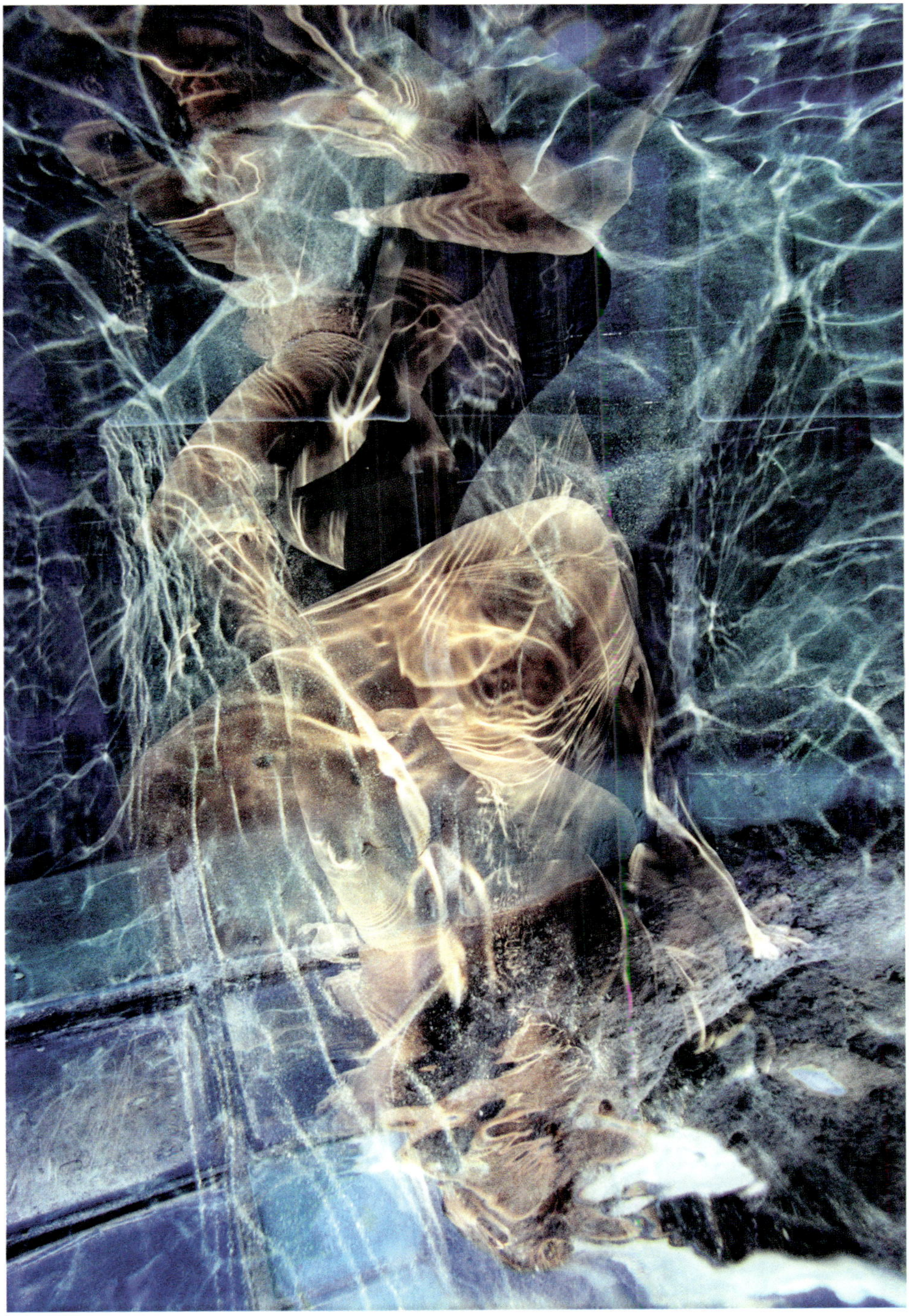

*Quandra Loka*, 2003.
Single Image.

*The living body inherently wants to realize,*
*or <u>be</u> one with, the matrix of life.*

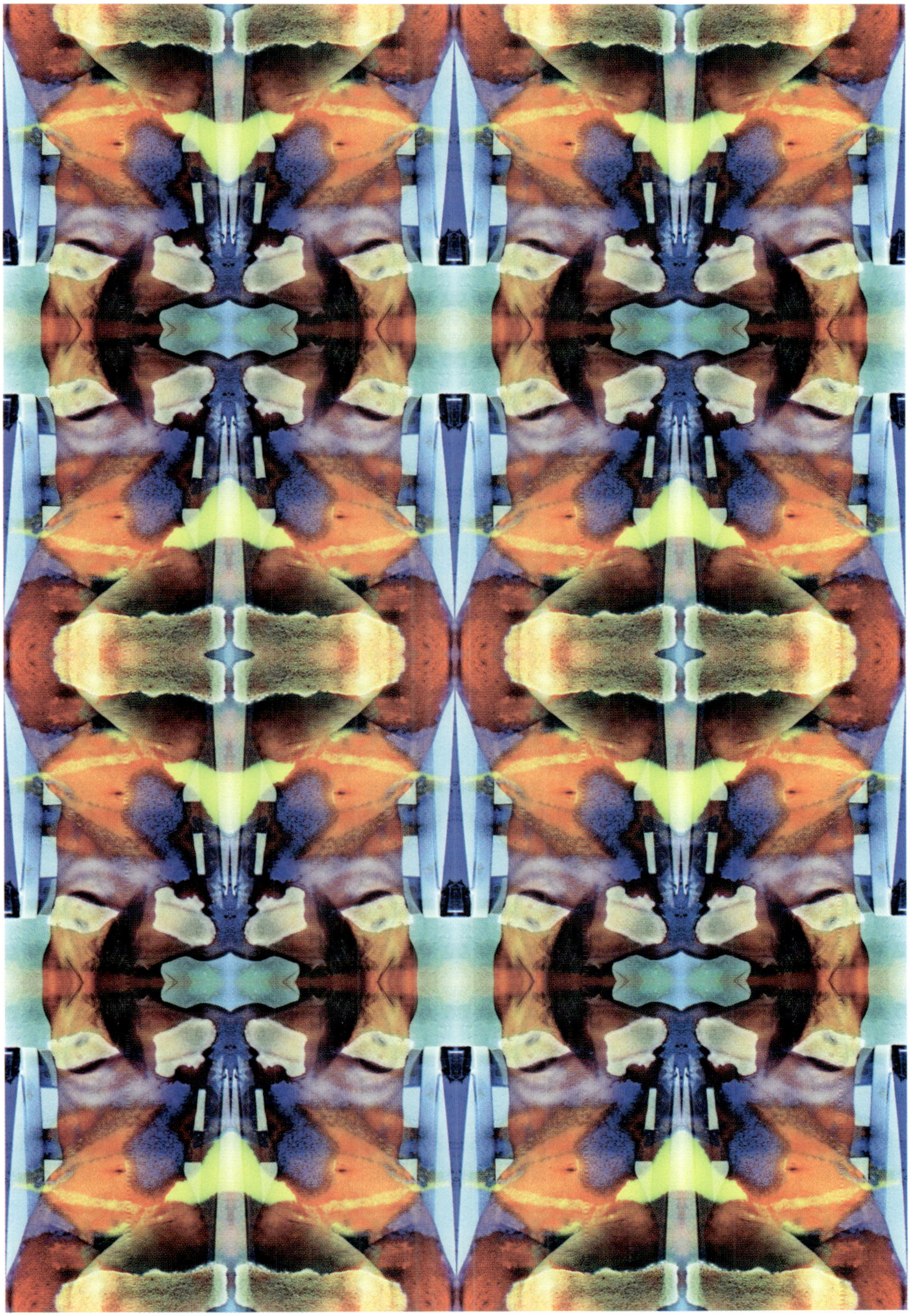

*Three*, 2003.
Complex Configuration.

*Ultimately, when "point of view" is transcended, there is no longer any "room", or any separate "location" and separate "self", at all—but only love-bliss-"brightness", limitlessly felt, in vast unpatterned joy.*

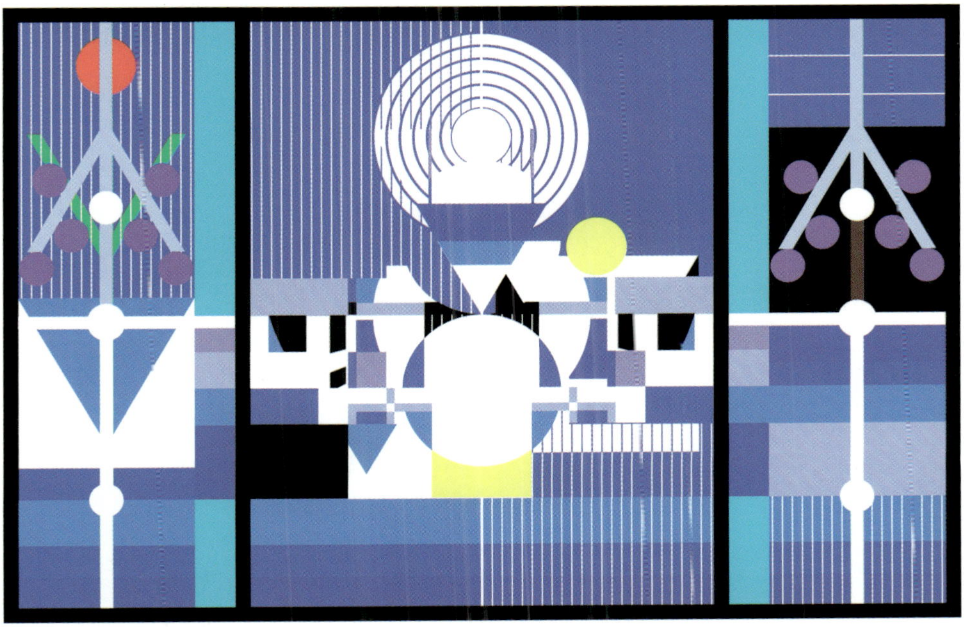

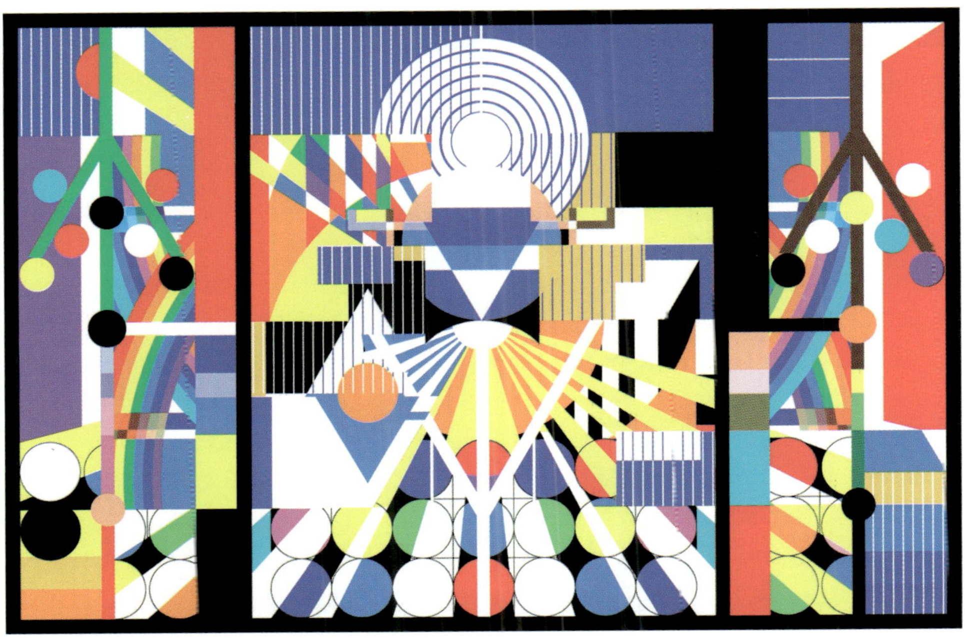

top: *The Order Of The Day: Saturday 1, 2006.*
bottom: *The Order Of The Day: Sunday 1, 2006.*
From *Geome One: Alberti's Window.*

# Adi Da Samraj

## The Master of the Transformational Art of Transcendental Realism

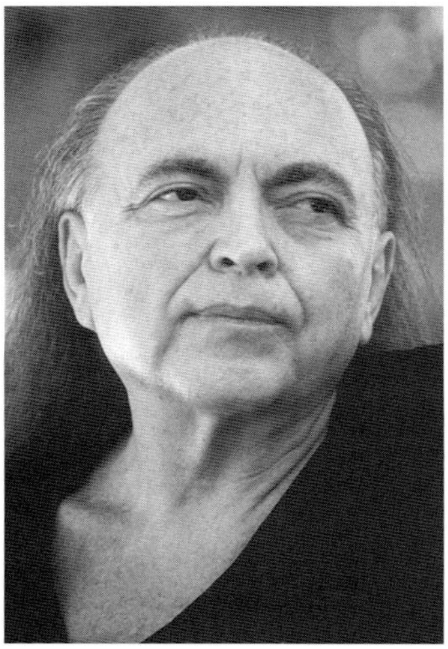

From his birth (on Long Island, New York, in 1939), Adi Da Samraj has always manifested unique signs of spiritual illumination and of artistic and literary inspiration. Nevertheless, from his birth, and until his spiritual restoration at thirty years of age, Adi Da Samraj submitted himself to an ordeal of "self-identification" with all the limitations and sufferings of the human condition.

Adi Da Samraj describes his early years as being focused in two fundamental activities: investigating how, in the scale of human "ordinariness", to perfectly realize the Truth of "Reality Itself", and (coincidently) both achieving and demonstrating the human-scale ability to communicate the Truth of "Reality Itself" through artistic means (both visual and literary).

Adi Da Samraj graduated from Columbia University in 1961, with a BA in philosophy (including much concentration in both art and literature), and from Stanford University in 1966, with an MA in English literature. His master's thesis, a study of core issues in modernism, focused on the literary experiments of Gertrude Stein and on the modernist painters of the same period.

In 1964, Adi Da Samraj began a period of intensive practice under a succession of spiritual masters in the United States and India. In 1968, he went to India, and approached the renowned spiritual master Swami Muktananda of Ganeshpuri, who immediately responded by saying that Adi Da Samraj was a spiritual master at birth, and "the most extraordinary Westerner" he (Swami Muktananda) had ever encountered. One year later, in a unique letter of acknowledgment, Swami Muktananda made an open public declaration that Adi Da Samraj is, by virtue of his evident spiritual signs and demonstrated states, inherently qualified to teach others independently, and to awaken others spiritually by direct transmission. Later, in 1970, after a final period of intense spiritual endeavor, Adi Da Samraj spontaneously became re-established in the continuous state of illumination that was his unique condition at birth—and that re-awakening signaled the end of his thirty years of spiritual quest.

After his re-awakening, Adi Da Samraj began to teach, creating a vast repository of wisdom, in living dialogue with those who approached him as devotees. To date, his literary, philosophical, and practical writings consist of over sixty published books—many internationally acclaimed. In the early 1970s, Alan Watts, writer of numerous books on religion and philosophy, acknowledged Adi Da Samraj as "a rare being", adding "It is obvious, from all sorts of subtle details, that he knows what IT's all about." In the late 1990s, poet Robert Lax said of Adi Da's radically experimental novel, *The Mummery Book* (the opening volume of Adi Da's *"First Room" Trilogy*), "Living and working as a writer for many decades, I have not encountered a book like this, that mysteriously and unselfconsciously conveys so much of the unspeakable reality."

Now, having fully given his teaching, Adi Da Samraj lives independently on his island-retreat in Fiji, where he constantly works to express the Truth of existence through modes of communication to which all human beings can respond—including literary, theatrical, and artistic works.



ABOUT THE AUTHOR: Mei-Ling Israel holds a degree in Modern Thought and Literature from Stanford University. Her research essay, *Seeking the Phoenix: Artistic Consciousness in the Nuclear Age*, is in the collection of the Museum of Modern Art library in New York City. She is a working glass artist and a published poet and playwright. From 2001–2004, she witnessed Adi Da's artistic process as an assistant and sometimes photographic subject.

## BOOKS ON THE ART OF ADI DA SAMRAJ

*THE BRIGHT FIELD:*
*The Photographic Art of Samraj Adi Da*

*THE* QUANDRA LOKA *SUITE: 52 VIEWS*
by Adi Da Samraj

*THE SPECTRA SUITES*
by Adi Da Samraj

*TRANSCENDENTAL REALISM:*
*The Art of Adi Da Samraj*
Catalogue of Collateral Exhibition at the 2007 Venice Biennale

*TRANSCENDENTAL REALISM:*
*The Image-Art of egoless Coincidence with Reality Itself*
Essays by Adi Da Samraj

---

For more information on the art of Adi Da Samraj,
or to order the above books and catalogues,
please contact:

Da Plastique™

**www.daplastique.com**

info@daplastique.com